SpringerBriefs in Climate Studies

SpringerBriefs in Climate Studies present concise summaries of cutting-edge research and practical applications. The series focuses on interdisciplinary aspects of Climate Science, including regional climate, climate monitoring and modeling, palaeoclimatology, as well as vulnerability, mitigation and adaptation to climate change. Featuring compact volumes of 50 to 125 pages (approx. 20,000–70,000 words), the series covers a range of content from professional to academic such as: a timely reports of state-of-the art analytical techniques, literature reviews, in-depth case studies, bridges between new research results, snapshots of hot and/or emerging topics Author Benefits: SpringerBriefs in Climate Studies allow authors to present their ideas and readers to absorb them with minimal time investment. Books in this series will be published as part of Springer's eBook collection, with millions of users worldwide. In addition, Briefs will be available for individual print and electronic purchase. SpringerBriefs books are characterized by fast, global electronic dissemination and standard publishing contracts. Books in the program will benefit from easy-to-use manuscript preparation and formatting guidelines, and expedited production schedules. Both solicited and unsolicited manuscripts are considered for publication in this series. Projects will be submitted to editorial review by editorial advisory boards and/or publishing editors. For a proposal document please contact the Publisher.

More information about this series at https://link.springer.com/bookseries/11581

Arjen Siegmann

Editor

Climate of the Middle

Understanding Climate Change
as a Common Challenge

 Springer

Editor
Arjen Siegmann
Vrije Universiteit Amsterdam
Amsterdam, Noord-Holland
The Netherlands

ISSN 2213-784X   ISSN 2213-7858 (electronic)
SpringerBriefs in Climate Studies
ISBN 978-3-030-85321-1   ISBN 978-3-030-85322-8 (eBook)
https://doi.org/10.1007/978-3-030-85322-8

This Springer imprint is published by the registered company Springer Nature Switzerland AG
The registered company address is: Gewerbestrasse 11, 6330 Cham, Switzerland

Preface

This volume brings together the insights of a number of scholars who each write from their own expertise about climate change and its consequences for society at large. Some of them are descriptive, explaining the most recent insights in human behaviour and perception of climate risks. Others have a more normative character, describing concrete ideas to address the climate challenge. I recommend the reader to approach both types of contributions as a stimulus to their own thinking.

Each chapter has been reviewed by an outside expert. They are, in alphabetical order, Dr Michel den Elzen, Prof Dr Peter Essers, Prof Dr Bert Jan Lietaert Peerbolte, Dr Bouke Klein Teeselink, Dr Jens van 't Klooster, Dr Gerard van der Meijden and Prof Dr Harmen Verbruggen. I am very much indebted to their willingness to spend time and provide their expertise on reviewing the chapters. From the Martens Centre, Gavin Synnott was very helpful in commenting on earlier versions of the text. Thanks to Margaret Deignan from Springer for creating the conditions to make this volume into an academic publication.

This publication receives funding from the European Parliament. The Wilfried Martens Centre for European Studies, the Wetenschappelijk Instituut voor het CDA (the co-organisers of this project) and the European Parliament assume no responsibility for facts or opinions expressed in this publication or any subsequent use of the information contained therein. Sole responsibility lies on the author of the publication. The publication was completed in 2020 and made available for Springer's Open Access platform in 2021.

Amsterdam, The Netherlands   Arjen Siegmann

Contents

Contributors

Wouter Botzen Institute for Environmental Studies (IVM), Vrije Universiteit Amsterdam & Utrecht University School of Economics, Amsterdam, The Netherlands

Francisco Estrada Universidad Nacional Autónoma de México & Vrije Universiteit, Amsterdam, The Netherlands

Jan Gooijer Faculty of Law, Vrije Universiteit Amsterdam, Amsterdam, The Netherlands

David Leiser Department of Psychology, Ben Gurion University, Beersheba, Israel

Dirk Schoenmaker Erasmus University, Bruegel & CEPR, Rotterdam, The Netherlands

Arjen Siegmann Vrije Universiteit Amsterdam, Amsterdam, Noord-Holland, The Netherlands

Hans von Storch Hamburg, Germany

Pascal Wagner-Egger Université de Fribourg, Fribourg, Switzerland

Chapter 1
Introduction and Lessons Learned

Arjen Siegmann

Abstract This chapter introduces the theme of the book and gives an overview of the lessons learned from the individual chapters.

1.1 Introduction

There is broad support for dealing with climate change. There is consensus among scientists, support among the population and international agreements have been concluded on a sharp reduction in emissions. However, there is still a long way to go, in which the way in which policy is implemented, the technical possibilities and affordability are constantly under discussion. An additional problem is the polarisation in the public debate, a sharpening of positions which generates media attention but makes it increasingly difficult to find the right middle ground.

For an effective and efficient transition towards a circular economy – a policy 'from the middle' – three questions will need to be answered. First, how do extreme opinions about climate change arise and how can we deal with them? Second, how do we balance the need for freedom and responsibility with the required level of coordination? Third, how can climate policy build on the existing norms and values in society? These questions form the starting point for the contributions in this volume.

For the purpose of this introductory chapter I describe the lessons from the contributions that have a bearing on the three questions above (polarisation, shared responsibility and morality). In doing so, I take some freedom of interpretation. Readers are encouraged to read the contributions themselves to draw their own conclusions.

A. Siegmann (✉)
Vrije Universiteit Amsterdam, Amsterdam, Noord-Holland, The Netherlands

Wetenschappelijk Instituut voor het CDA, Den Haag, The Netherlands
e-mail: a.h.siegmann@vu.nl

A. Siegmann (ed.), *Climate of the Middle*, SpringerBriefs in Climate Studies,
https://doi.org/10.1007/978-3-030-85322-8_1

1.2   Dealing with Polarised Positions on Climate Change

With the arrival of the internet and free access to almost all of the world's information, one could have expected that people are now better informed than ever. Whether we are, we do not exactly know. But we do observe that over some issues, such as climate change, positions are quite polarised. And, more importantly, the polarisation does not seem to be a problem of information. It is more prominent under the highly educated, a problem of perception rather than information, and related to the fat-tailed and complex nature of climate change events.

Polarisation Is More Prominent Among the Highly Educated
Motivated reasoning is one of the root causes that leads to polarised positions. This implies that people who think they are better at 'reasoning' are more prone to confirmation bias: evidence is taken into account to the extent that it fits with prior beliefs. David Leiser cites the research that shows this on many topics, but clearly on the issue of climate change: the more highly people are educated, the more prominent the polarisation on climate change is.

This fact holds a lesson for all those concerned with the environment: more information, education or government education might result in increased polarisation, and not in less. Communication has no effect on those who are already convinced. And those who are convinced of an alternative will not change their mind. Even worse, they will start to consider the increase in information as propaganda. As Peter Drucker notes in his book on the eve of the second world war: "Yet it is as true today as it ever was that propaganda only converts those who already believe". (Drucker, 1939).

Some polarisation on the issue of climate change has been intentional: some conservative or centre-right parties have been very reluctant in accepting climate change as an important problem (Carrus et al., 2018). Although possibly motivated by the fear of anarchist tendencies, the effect of framing climate change activists as 'radicals' have played into the hands of those groups that are now seen as a threat to Western democracy, i.e., conspiracy thinkers.

As shown by David Leiser in this volume, conspiracy-style thinking has become more and more pervasive in the Western world. It is a style of thinking that is usually connected to a distrust in public institutions, most notably the government. It can sometimes be born out of boredom,[1] or out of scepticism, but can just as well be weaponized by terror groups and state actors to destabilize free and democratic countries.

Biases in Perception Make Climate Risks Hard to Incorporate in Daily Life
People's perceptions of climate change affects the way they express themselves in public and, more importantly, at the ballot box. In this volume, Wouter Botzen

---

[1] As in "Is QAnon a game gone wrong?" an FT Film, October 15, 2020. Available at https://www.youtube.com/watch?v=-4vb6UWhf3o

describes biases in how people arrive at perceptions of climate change, and how that leads to unnecessary polarisation.

The biases are those of simplification, availability, finite pool of worry and myopia. Simplification means that very small risks are simplified into a category of negligible risks that need no further concern. The availability bias makes people assess only those risks for which events are available to them in living memory. A finite pool of worry limits the number of problems that people assess as warranting attention. Finally, myopia (short-sightedness) shortens the time horizon at which people assess risks. These four biases work against a realistic assessment of climate risks.

Communication strategies and the framing of climate policy should take into account the existence of these biases. The chapter of Botzen details these, such as communicating climate risks in a way that is simpler and in proportion to other life experiences that we have. The price mechanism is another way of making sure that people can make decisions that take climate considerations into account. For example, it would be quite helpful if the reduction in CO_2 that comes with home isolation or energy saving investments would be quantified as such. Doing this requires some effort from governments, but would add to the credibility of policies that are advocating personal responsibility.

A contributing factor to problems of perception is that of personal values. The beliefs and unbeliefs in the realities of climate change seem to be related to values that people have. Those with individual and hierarchical values tend to be more sceptic. Those with egalitarian and communitarian values are less sceptic. As a consequence, a reasoned approach to climate change should avoid a shallow framing of the problem. Graham et al. (2009) and Haidt (2012) warn of the framing of political issues in terms of an 'individualizing' cluster of values, such as care and fairness. This leaves out the group-focused cluster of 'binding' values, such as loyalty, authority and sanctity.

An Interplay of Predictable Risks

Climate change risks are extremely difficult to assess for anyone. And even if they are properly assessed, the materialization of risks can be misleading. The reason is that the distribution of extreme weather outcomes, or disasters, is typically fat-tailed: it does not follow the normal Gaussian distribution of outcomes. Shoe sizes, heights and IQ are all Gaussian distributed, which makes measurement of a small sample representative for the whole population. Heavy-tailed distributions are the opposite, which makes a small no-risk sample quite misleading: the absence of events does not imply an absent risk. Rather, it suggests that risky events, if they occur, will be large.

In this volume, Francisco Estrada makes the point that climate risks are heavy-tailed because they come from the interplay between more predictable trends. We know that the temperature rises and it is easy to see this as a 'normal' process: like the temperature falls and rises over the course of the seasons. But it is misleading because the global rise in temperatures interacts with other processes, like ice formation on the Antarctic continent. It is the interaction between several well-known, predictable processes, that leads to unpredictable events.

It is the nature of catastrophic events that makes climate change policies a hard political problem: the absent of catastrophes cannot be claimed as a political 'win', as it says nothing about the underlying likelihood of extreme events. It forces politicians to be more authentic in the underlying 'matter' (Taylor, 1992) and be less concerned with the mood of the moment.

1.3 Achieving a Good Distribution of Responsibilities

Climate action cannot be limited to government policies. If our economies ever become climate neutral, it will be because households and firms have innovated, invested and consumed in different ways than they currently do. This is the perspective of 'subsidiarity': the idea that responsibility is best laid at the lowest hierarchical level. Subsidiarity is a conviction that people thrive in an environment where there is a clear and simple relationship between their own actions and the results of those actions.

The principle is mentioned as such in the Treaty on European Union (1992) and extended in the Treaty of Amsterdam (1997) to be used in the assessment of legislative proposals. In this form, subsidiarity is a bulwark against instrumentalism and an overbearing bureaucracy.

A good distribution of responsibilities leads to economic efficiency. Efficiency means that we reduce greenhouse gases at the lowest cost possible. It is a necessary condition for a sustainable economic model for which moral convictions are, by themselves, not enough. As Bowles and Carlin (2020) write: "Successful policy paradigms combine a set of ethical values with a model of how the economy works, a property of which is that the pursuit of those ethical values contributes to the performance of the economy as represented in the model."

There is also an existential reason for devolving responsibilities: a sustained effort to better the world needs ample room for joy, curiosity and cooperation. Joy is the expression of doing something that is worthwhile and that draws on our abilities to overcome hurdles, to work together with other people. In this cooperation, we learn from each other, experience human relationships, mutual help, reciprocity and love. It is a necessary ingredient of meaningful life and it comes to us when there is room for initiative and freedom. Without it, climate change action risks becoming a joyless and bureaucratic affair.

In this section, I describe the lessons from the following chapters as follows: Firms and households alike would benefit from easier-to-access facts about carbon prices and the value of their contribution. For companies to take on their own responsibility, taxation could evolve to be more friendly to a circular form of production. Financial markets should price the risks of unsustainable business practices correctly. And countries could muster the national pride and sense of direction by formulating difficult technical challenges as 'Apollo projects'.

An Arbiter of Facts as a Form of Climate Policy

Households and firms have a hard time gauging the realities of climate change and their role in mitigating greenhouse gas emissions. Large firms in Europe have the emissions trading scheme (ETS), the rest of us have nothing. That is, we might receive well-intended communication about subsidy schemes, energy savings plans and the possibilities of investing in clean energy. But what we – the public – lack is a clear *quantification* of the size of the contribution that is needed.

As Von Storch writes in his contribution, most of the middle class is keen on acting against the potentially catastrophic effects of climate change. However, it lacks trustworthy estimates of the size of the challenge, and the role it can play in it. To stimulate political responsibility and accountability, the public needs cost-benefit analyses of climate policies, both in terms of money and of emissions.

Possibilities for a Green Corporate Tax

The legal structure of the corporation is a unique invention, as a place where people work together for a common goal. It brings together labour, capital and entrepreneurship in a way that is beneficial to all the partners. In his contribution, Jan Gooijer describes the reasons for corporate taxation, next to personal income taxes and value-added taxes. From the theory of taxation, a clear rationale emerges for basing some of the tax rules on the extent of circularity of the company.

Currently, corporate taxes do not discriminate on whether the firm pollutes, uses many or little resources, or performs any function in transitioning towards a more sustainable economy. Instead, they could better differentiate between business practices that are sustainable and those that are not. Criteria have been developed that are a good starting point for a 'greener' corporate tax. For large corporations, the relevant data is already in place by 2022. For smaller and medium-sized enterprises, practical solutions still have to be developed.

The Market Can Be Wrong: A Role for the Central Bank

The information problem about climate change cannot be solved by centralized planning. As Hayek (1945) points out in his famous essay *The use of knowledge in society*, there is simply not enough power of mind and coordination to understand and influence the actions and interactions of millions of people. It is the price mechanism that performs this role, almost magically, by letting the individual actions of consumers and producers be displayed in the prices of goods and services. This mechanism should and does work for the challenge of reducing greenhouse gases.

However, devolving responsibility to the market for assessing the seriousness of climate change or the shadow price of climate action has pitfalls. As Dirk Schoenmaker points out in his contribution, markets have been spectacularly wrong before. One only has to think of the statement of former Fed-governor, Alan Greenspan, to Congress, after the derivative market collapsed in 2008: "I made a mistake in presuming that the self-interests of organisations, specifically banks and others, were such that they were best capable of protecting their own shareholders and their equity in the firms"(Clark & Treanor, 2008). And this meant that a theory was wrong that he had held dear for a long, namely that of efficient markets.

Markets could be wrong again, especially in how they value traditional, polluting businesses. Climate neutrality by 2050 requires that not all proven reserves of carbohydrates are mined. Investors, however, are still pricing in the value of proven reserves, see Livsey (2020).

Given the imperfections in how investors assess climate risks, and the potential tipping points in the climate, Schoenmaker argues for a larger role of the ECB. The ECB could incorporate a sustainable outlook in their operations, such as in a Green-QE program. This could be one way of influencing the markets and preventing an "I was wrong" statement by the then-ECB president in 2030.

For a good distribution of responsibilities, a clear mandate from the EU on this topic would be essential. Its current mandate is not sufficient to fully take on the responsibilities for a "Green QE" operation. Political action is required.

Apollo Projects as Stimulators of Innovation

The climate change challenge is in the gigaton-range. This scale of emission reductions is not in a range that is comprehensible by ordinary households or small and medium enterprises. This scale needs to be in proportion to the scale from which solutions can be expected. Energy savings plans and relying on current technology will just not do enough. What is needed are incentives, prizes or an appeal to national pride to develop breakthrough technologies.

The public is keen on acting against the potentially catastrophic effects of climate change. However, the effects of individual action, or even those of groups of people, can be very disappointing in terms of emissions reductions. This inconvenient fact is the starting point for the contribution of Hans von Storch. His contribution connects the goodwill of people and the thrill of exploration to what is needed for a long-term solution to halt or reverse anthropogenic climate change.

In this volume, Hans von Storch lists the breakthroughs that are not just nice-to-have, but essential and required for developed economies being net-carbon-neutral in 2050: cheap and high-capacity storage of electricity, sources of green energy, carbon capture and sequestration, emission-free ship propulsion. And so on. Von Storch calls these projects 'Apollo projects' that should appeal to national pride and to working towards something, not because it is easy, but because it is hard.

It is an appealing and joyful prospect to set high goals. It connects the goodwill of people and the thrill of exploration to what is needed for a long-term solution to halt or reverse anthropogenic climate change. It reminds us of the Ansari X Prize for incentivizing the creation of a reliable, reusable, privately financed, crewed spaceship. Innovation is helped by unleashing forms of competition, a variety of motivators and well-designed goals (Wagner, 2011). A similar momentous effort was the race to map the whole human genome in 2000, or the race to create a vaccine for the worldwide Covid-19 pandemic in 2020. In the latter case, a previously unheard of time of just 9 months, technology, entrepreneurship and politics came together to solve a global issue. This approach should inspire governments everywhere to set ambitious goals for technological breakthroughs that are needed. It is also rooted in the normal inclinations of people to seek novelty, cooperation and marvel at new discoveries.

1.4 Building on Existing Moral Inclinations

Humans have an inbuilt sense of right and wrong. And, since companies are made up of people, we can expect them to have a corporate moral responsibility. The cases of wrongdoing, both by individuals and by firms are the exceptions that prove the rule: evil needs to be punished. Without having to digress into natural law, we can state that climate change policies can build on existing moral imperatives.

Morality can change, and does change over time. This is the democratic element of ethics: there are things that we consider 'right', just because everybody around us believes so. This is a process of cultural development and should be respected as such.

It is in this sphere of cultural change that many climate change proposals are sometimes proposed: people should eat less meat, fly less, and have a smaller environmental footprint. This can be counterproductive. Mostly, because it presupposes that cultural norms can be changed at whim. They do not. And even if they could, we should be wary of grand schemes to try to change cultural norms in the direction of who happens to be in power (Dikötter, 2016).

Work with Biases, Not Against Them
In Chap. 2, Wouter Botzen classifies five types of biases that are relevant for people's attitudes towards climate change. They are the biases of simplification, availability, a finite pool of worry, myopia (short sightedness) and herding. The complexity of the climate problem does not lend itself to a simple cause-and-effect relationship or personal experience of the problem at hand. This limits the possibility for understanding the problems at hand, let alone to convince voters.

At the same time, the biases are nothing new for the politically inclined: since the beginning of time, political communication and strategy have made use of the heuristics and biases that people use to observe the outside world. The overarching theme for political action is that of framing: the deliberate action of associating a certain cause with elements that appeal to voters. It is in the framing that we should acknowledge moral imperatives and be wary of framing it in a way that only appeals to the interested sub-group. As Botzen writes: "A broader willingness to contribute to solving this problem, based on intrinsic motivations, is urgently needed if policymakers aim to rapidly transit to a low-carbon economy."

A Legal Basis for Greening Corporate Taxation
If we want corporations' interests to be aligned with the goal of a more circular economy, the tax code is a potential factor for change. But at the same time, taxation should adhere to sound principles and not have an ad hoc character. In his contribution, Jan Gooijer, describes the rationale for corporate taxation as that of privileged acquisition, balance of power and that of the damage and well-being principle. Within these principles he finds enough traction for fiscal rules that take into account the sustainability of company real estate and an interest rate deductibility that takes into account the environmental impact of production.

1.5 Conclusion

Climate change can only become a common challenge if we move beyond polarised positions, have a clear distribution of responsibilities and build on the moral inclinations that are present or develop from the population at large. From this conviction, this chapter has tried to summarize the main lessons from the contributions in this book along the lines of the three aspects.

Polarisation is at first a problem of knowledge and perception, and made worse by the complex nature of climate change. Paradoxically, polarised positions are more clearly seen under highly educated people. It seems to vindicate David Hume's aphorism that *reason is a slave to the passions*. Policy makers should be aware of this problem and not expect too much from communication and information. Moreover, political strategies that downplay scientific facts or concerns could backfire in being supportive of conspiracy-style thinkers.

A distinct separation of responsibilities is crucial for efficiency and sense of responsibility of households and firms. A green corporate tax exemplifies the responsibilities of the corporate sector. A proper market for waste make circularity possible. Information about carbon prices and the efficiency gains of technologies are needed for firms and households to take their own initiative. The importance of a functioning ETS market for carbon emissions cannot be overstated, but there remain market failures that could be addressed by the ECB. For the ECB to act on that, however, it first needs a clear mandate in its charter.

Finally, incorporating a view on existing morals should not be a high-brow exercise in virtue signalling but a way of bridging antagonistic positions. It is the existing polarisation that should teach us to bridge divides and find a middle ground. And there are enough leads for finding a middle ground: we can avoid working against behavioural biases. Green corporate taxation can be based on existing legal grounds. Apollo projects can appeal to our sense of national pride in a positive way and stimulate joyful innovation. That would constitute a good 'climate of the middle'.

References

Bowles, S., & Carlin, W. (2020). Shrinking capitalism. *AEA Papers and Proceedings, 110*, 372–377.

Carrus, G., Panno, A., & Leone, L. (2018). The moderating role of interest in politics on the relations between conservative political orientation and denial of climate change. *Society & Natural Resources, 31*(10), 1103–1117.

Clark, A, & Treanor, J. (2008). Greenspan–I was wrong about the economy. Sort of. *The Guardian* 24.

Dikötter, F. (2016). *The cultural revolution: A people's history, 1962–1976*. Bloomsbury Publishing USA.

Drucker, P. F. (1939). *The end of economic man: The origins of totalitarianism*. Transaction Publishers; Revised edition (January 30, 1995).

Graham, J., Haidt, J., & Nosek, B. A. (2009). Liberals and conservatives rely on different sets of moral foundations. *Journal of Personality and Social Psychology, 96*(5), 1029.

Haidt, J. (2012). *The righteous mind: Why good people are divided by politics and religion.* Vintage.

Hayek, F. A. (1945). The use of knowledge in society. *The American Economic Review, 35*(4), 519–530.

Livsey, A. (2020). Lex in depth: The $900 bn cost of 'stranded energy assets'. *Financial Times* February 4, 2020.

Taylor, C. (1992). *The ethics of authenticity.* Harvard University Press.

Wagner, E. B. (2011). Why prize? The surprising resurgence of prizes to stimulate innovation. *Research-Technology Management, 54*(6), 32–36.

Arjen Siegmann is research asssociate at the CDA Research Institute ("Wetenschappelijk Instituut voor het CDA"), associate professor of finance at the Vrije Universiteit Amsterdam and member of the executive board of the Wilfried Martens Centre for Economic Studies. He has written reports on long-term unemployment, the housing market and fiscal policy. In common projects with the Martens Centre and the Konrad Adenauer Foundation, he has edited two books on the Middle Class in Europe. His academic research and teaching focuses on financial markets and institutions. He has been a council member at the city of Amstelveen, a researcher at the Netherlands Central Bank (DNB) and an advisor on strategic model development at Abn Amro Bank.

Chapter 2
Perceptions of Catastrophic Climate Risks

Wouter Botzen

Abstract Many climate change-related risks, such as more frequent and severe natural disasters, can be characterised as low-probability/high-consequence (LP/HC) events. Perceptions of LP/HC risks are often associated with biases which hamper taking action to limit these risks, such as underestimation of risk, myopia, and the adoption of simplified decision heuristics. This chapter discusses these biases and outlines key elements of policies to overcome them in order to enhance climate action.

2.1 Introduction

Climate change is projected to have severe societal impacts and economic consequences around the world (IPCC, 2014). The consequences of climate change are far reaching and will be experienced by a large diversity of economic sectors and population groups. For example, these consequences encompass increases in the frequency and/or severity of various extreme weather events and related losses from natural disasters in many regions around the world (IPCC, 2012; Botzen et al., 2019a). Moreover, climate change is expected to have impacts on human health as well as on the agriculture, tourism, industry, and financial sectors (Tol, 2018).

Since at least part of the climate change caused by increasing concentrations of greenhouse gases in the atmosphere can no longer be avoided, climate change adaptation policies and measures must be put in place to limit societal impacts from the aspects of global warming that will inevitably occur (Mauritsen & Pincus, 2017). If around the world stringent climate policies are implemented in the coming years to drastically reduce greenhouse gas emissions, then there is still a chance that global warming can be limited to meet the objectives outlined in the 2015 Paris Agreement to keep the global average temperature rise to well below 2 °C above pre-industrial

W. Botzen (✉)
Institute for Environmental Studies (IVM), Vrije Universiteit Amsterdam & Utrecht
University School of Economics, Amsterdam, The Netherlands
e-mail: wouter.botzen@vu.nl

© The Author(s) 2022
A. Siegmann (ed.), *Climate of the Middle*, SpringerBriefs in Climate Studies,
https://doi.org/10.1007/978-3-030-85322-8_2

11

levels (IPCC, 2018). However, this objective can only be met if current climate change mitigation policies become much more ambitious around the world as there are large gaps between countries' intentions to reduce greenhouse gas emissions and what is actually needed to meet the Paris targets (Rogelj et al., 2016). The required reductions in greenhouse gas emissions imply that a fundamental transformation of consumption and production processes is needed to move towards a low-carbon economy which produces net zero emissions between 2040 and 2050 (IPCC, 2018).

Section 2.1 explains why perceptions of catastrophic risks matter. Section 2.2 discusses several of the main biases which influence perceptions of risks associated with climate change and impact individual decision making about climate change mitigation and adaptation actions. This is followed in Sect. 2.3 by a discussion of climate policy strategies which work with, instead of against, these behavioural biases to stimulate climate action. Section 2.4 concludes.

2.2 Why Perceptions of Climate Risks Matter

The diversity of climate change impacts for which adaptation measures are needed and the systemic changes required to successfully move towards a low-carbon economy imply that a large variety of actors should be involved in climate change adaptation and mitigation strategies. Each of these actors, such as firms, households, and governments, have different roles to play with distinct responsibilities. For instance, in climate change mitigation policies which aim to reduce greenhouse gas emissions, governments have a central role in designing and enforcing regulations and putting a price on carbon, either through carbon taxes or emission trading systems. The reason is that the public good nature of the atmosphere implies there are strong incentives for companies and individuals to free ride on emission reductions by others, whilst problems with carbon leakage and rebound effects of energy savings also imply that voluntary action by individuals and firms is unlikely to be effective in solving climate change (van den Bergh et al., 2020).

However, in the end it are the individual households and firms who should take the required steps and measures to reduce emissions and improve energy efficiency, such as switching to renewable energy. Moreover, the implementation of stringent climate policy measures by the public sector is likely to depend on the support of voters and lobbying by firms.

Since climate change is a global issue, not only is action by national governments needed, but international collaboration is critical (Nordhaus, 2015). Regarding climate change adaptation policies, governments are crucial in the financing or provision of measures related to the public good, such as improved infrastructure for flood protection. Furthermore, governments are well positioned to enforce regulations such as building codes which enhance resilience to extreme weather, and they can, for example, guide adaptation practises, like agricultural policies, through subsidies. Adaptation measures that limit impacts from climate chance often bring private benefits by lowering risks for households, farmers and companies that implement these measures. This implies that these private agents also have a responsibility and financial interest in limiting the climate change risks they face, for instance, by taking steps to reduce damage to their properties from natural disasters and obtaining financial protection by purchasing insurance against these risks.

Therefore, individual perceptions of the risks associated with climate change are likely to be an important driver of support for adaptation and mitigation policies and to influence the actions individuals take to prevent or mitigate the impacts of global warming. Many of these climate change-related risks, such as more frequent and severe natural disasters, can be characterised as low-probability/high-consequence (LP/HC) events. Decades of research in psychology and behavioural economics have shown that individuals have challenges understanding LP/HC risks and that they do not necessarily perceive them the same way an expert would (Slovic, 2000). Individual decision making about LP/HC climate change risks appears to be based on simplified decision heuristics, and individual behaviour is found to be associated with systematic biases which hamper being adequately prepared for these risks (Kahneman, 2011; Meyer & Kunreuther, 2017). The presence of such biases is supported by studies showing that individual perceptions of LP/HC risks associated with climate change systematically deviate from expert assessments of these risks (Botzen et al., 2015; Mol et al., 2020).

Many residents of disaster-prone areas fail to take cost-effective measures to limit the impacts of these disasters and do not purchase insurance against these risks, even when premiums are close to actuarially fair levels or subsidized (Kunreuther, 1996; Botzen, 2013). These observations conflict with principles of economic rationality, and highlight the need to understand behavioural biases that lead to suboptimal preparedness for climate change to guide the design of effective climate policy.

2.3 Biases and Heuristics in Decision-Making

Suboptimal climate action may be explained by insufficient support for climate policy that is related to climate change perceptions, a lack of individual support for the common good by insufficiently reducing one's own carbon footprint, and a failure to adequately prepare for risks associated with climate change, such as natural disasters. This section starts with the first topic that is often related to support for public sector climate policy, although individual perceptions of climate change also influence their own actions to reduce greenhouse gas emissions and adapt to climate change impacts.

Although awareness about climate change has generally increased around the world during the last several decades, perceptions amongst citizens are not always in line with expert consensus (Capstick et al., 2015). This is, for instance, due to the presence of a large group of so-called climate sceptics (Whitmarsh, 2013). Many studies have examined how perceptions of climate change differ amongst sub-groups of the population, showing, for example, that political affiliation is an important determinant, with more conservative individuals having lower perceptions of climate change-related risks than liberals do (e.g. Botzen et al., 2016). This may be caused by differences in underlying individual values, ideologies, and worldviews which influence attitudes towards climate change.

A meta-analysis of the literature on this topic by Hornsey et al. (2016) discusses empirical evidence for these drivers of climate change perceptions. In particular, they show that individuals who place a high importance on the natural environment are more likely to believe that climate change is real. With regard to cultural aspects, people with relatively individualistic and hierarchical values prefer the status quo and are likely to doubt that industry threatens the environment, meaning they do not believe in climate change (Hornsey et al., 2016). Opposite beliefs that industry does pose a threat are held by people with egalitarian and communitarian values (Hornsey et al., 2016). Moreover, climate change scepticism has been associated with free market ideologies (Heath & Gifford, 2006). These individual beliefs in climate change are likely to influence public support for climate change mitigation policies; however, understanding their underlying causes can aid in the design of communication messages which enhance this support (Sect. 2.3).

Moreover, individual support for adaptation measures, and actors' willingness to take such steps to limit the impacts of climate change, is likely to depend on people's perceptions of specific risks associated with climate change, such as natural disasters. A substantial body of literature has shown that individuals have difficulties understanding and processing information about low-probability/high-consequence (LP/HC) risks (Kunreuther et al., 2001). This also applies to risks associated with climate change, such as the probability of and losses due to natural disasters. As an illustration, Botzen et al. (2015) and Mol et al. (2020) have compared individual perceptions of the probability of and the potential damage from flooding regarding households in flood-prone areas in the United States and the Netherlands, respectively. They have observed that even when an error margin of 50% is allowed, less than 25% have correct perceptions of the flood probability, and about 50% or fewer individuals have correct perceptions of potential flood damage. Underestimation of natural disaster risks is commonly viewed both as an explanation for a failure to take cost-effective risk-reduction measures by inhabitants of areas prone to natural disasters (Kunreuther, 1996) and as an obstacle to implementing climate change adaptation measures (van Valkengoed & Steg, 2019). This observed lack of disaster preparedness conflicts with principles of economic rationality of welfare maximizing agents. Individuals appear to regret not taking preparedness actions before disasters occur, since after personally experiencing a natural disaster people change their behaviour and start taking measures to limit impacts from future disasters (Bubeck et al., 2012). Individual perceptions of LP/HC risks and decision-making processes about these risks are associated with biases and heuristics, which can explain a lack of action to reduce impacts from LP/HC events before they occur. Here, I discuss some of the main biases which contribute to insufficient preparedness for risks associated with climate change and may hamper climate change mitigation actions. These can be categorised as simplification, availability, finite pool of worry, myopia, and herding (Kunreuther, 2018; Botzen et al., 2021).

Simplification Instead of making rational assessments of the full distribution of risks which individuals face, many people tend to simplify their assessments of risks due to bounded rationality and limited cognitive abilities to process them. For instance, many people tend to treat low probabilities as being zero, which implies that they do not consider taking action to reduce the risks. Others tend to overweigh low probabilities in decision making because they are concerned or worried about the risks. This behaviour is consistent with the application of threshold models, in which individuals judge whether a probability is below or above a threshold level of concern (Slovic et al., 1977). Because many risks associated with climate change, such as natural disasters, are LP/HC risks, individuals simplify this low probability to being zero or falling below their threshold level of concern, meaning no risk-reduction action is undertaken (Robinson & Botzen, 2018, 2019).

Availability Many individuals tend to underestimate LP/HC events unless they have personally experienced one, such as a natural disaster. This behaviour is caused by the availability heuristic, which postulates that individuals find it difficult to imagine a disaster occurring if they have not experienced it before (Tversky & Kahneman, 1973). In contrast, after people personally experienced a disaster, they can more easily imagine that it can happen to them again in the future. There is broad empirical support for this availability bias in the context of natural disaster risks by showing that individual perceptions of them (Kellens et al., 2013), as well as preparedness for future natural disasters (Bubeck et al., 2012; Osberghaus, 2017), increase after such a disaster occurs. However, since the probability that an individual personally experiences a disaster is low, the availability bias may contribute to underestimation of natural disaster risks amongst the majority of the population.

Finite Pool of Worry The finite pool of worry means that individuals cannot worry about too many risks at the same time (Capstick et al., 2015). This implies that if concern about one kind of risk increases, concern about other kinds of risks reduces. For instance, substantial declines in concern about climate change were observed in Europe after the 2008 financial crisis and its aftermath, when worries about employment increased (Duijndam & van Beukering, 2020). Given the large health and economic consequences of the current COVID-19 pandemic, the finite pool of worry is likely to result in decreased concern about risks associated with climate change once individuals become more concerned about health and unemployment (Botzen et al., 2021). As a consequence, support for climate policy and individual willingness to take climate change mitigation and adaptation measures is likely to go down.

Myopia Climate change adaptation and mitigation measures often have high upfront costs, as well as benefits which accrue over time in terms of lower risks or savings on energy bills. Individuals are less likely to invest in these measures if they have short time horizons over which they value future benefits and/or they heavily discount these benefits, meaning they weigh less in current decisions (Gillingham & Palmer, 2014; Botzen et al., 2019b; Gelino & Reed, 2020). This myopic behaviour is especially problematic with climate change, which is often not considered to be salient and rather viewed as a long-term problem. Myopia has the effect that people focus on near-term risks and neglect long-term risks, for which action is delayed. However, a dangerous feature of climate change is that once undesirable catastrophic impacts occur in the future, it may be too late to reverse global warming due to inertia in the climate system.

Herding Under conditions of uncertainty, such as benefits from climate change mitigation or adaptation, individual choices are guided by the behaviour of others. This has been called the herding bias and may be caused by the presence of social norms (Meyer & Kunreuther, 2017). Herding has been observed in individual decisions to prepare for natural disaster risks since individuals are more likely to take measures which limit disaster damage if they know others, like family, friends, or neighbours, have also taken such steps (Bubeck et al., 2013). Moreover, a large body of literature has shown that energy-savings measures are guided by social norms (Frederiks et al., 2015). The herding bias may also indicate fewer climate actions if individuals do not know others in their close social peer group who have taken adaptation and mitigation measures, which is likely given the lack of climate change action implied by the other aforementioned behavioural biases.

2.4 Policies that Work With—Not Against— Behavioral Biases

Effective climate policy strategies should be carefully designed to work with, instead of against, individual risk perceptions and behavioural biases. This can be achieved by a broad package of climate policy measures which combine communication strategies with regulations, financial incentives, and choice architecture (also called behavioural nudges). This section outlines the key elements to be included in such a strategy.

Communication strategies can contribute to building support for climate change adaptation and mitigation policies implemented by the public sector and create awareness about the risks and consequences of climate change to stimulate individual action. Support by citizens for climate change policies may be enhanced by working with individual ideologies and worldviews. Examples are framing pro-environmental climate change policies as a form of patriotism (Feygina et al., 2010) and communicating that transitions to renewable energy are investments in green technology (Bain et al., 2012) and also enhance national energy security (Gromet et al., 2013). These kinds of communication messages can also appeal to individuals with conservative ideologies and individualistic values who otherwise tend to oppose climate policy.

Furthermore, communication strategies should focus on overcoming the behavioural biases which prevent individuals from adequately preparing for risks associated with climate change, such as natural disasters. To overcome the simplification bias for people who treat low probabilities of experiencing a disaster as zero, communication strategies could frame low probabilities over long time horizons so individuals are less likely to perceive these risks as being below their threshold level of concern. For example, communicating the probability of flooding over a longer time horizon (e.g. a one in four chance of a flood in 30 years) instead of an annual time horizon (a one in 100 chance of a flood per year) can increase demand for protective measures against flooding (Botzen et al., 2016; Chaudhry et al., 2020). Empirical evidence has also shown that communicating the consequences of not preparing for climate change risks, such as the damage one would experience from a flood, can make people pay attention to the risk and demand protection against it (Bradt, 2019). Focussing on such worst-case scenarios may trigger individual concern for a risk and overcome the simplification bias.

A more general recommendation which goes beyond raising awareness of natural disaster risks is to stress health consequences from climate change in communication strategies. The reason is that health risks are salient to people and, for example, were a main cause of the broad public support for the Montreal Protocol to prevent ozone depletion (Pillay & van den Bergh, 2016). Moreover, stressing the link between pandemics and climate change may overcome declining concerns about climate change when worries about health risks increase (due to the current COVID-19 pandemic). This can address the finite pool of worry (Botzen et al., 2021). Climate change and pandemic risks are interlinked since several of the causes of the current pandemic (e.g. unsustainable transport, tourism, and food systems) also contribute to global warming, whilst climate change itself may increase the risks of infectious diseases and pandemics (IPCC, 2014). Creating awareness of this link amongst the general population may cause people to pay more attention to climate change in addition to pandemic risks (which are currently weighing heavily on the public's mind due to the availability bias). Once the memory of experiencing pandemics or natural disasters fades over time, communication policies can work with the availability bias by keeping the memory of such past disasters alive (Garde-Hansen et al., 2017).

To work with the herding bias, communication policies can focus on triggering social norms about energy efficiency and implementing adaptation measures such as preparing for natural disasters. Such social norm nudges can, for instance, inform people about climate change actions undertaken by others or be triggered by giving a seal of approval after certified inspections confirmed that people have taken measures which contribute to climate change mitigation or adaptation (Meyer & Kunreuther, 2017). Regulations and financial incentives can help in ensuring that a sufficient critical mass of people take climate actions, which can be spread further amongst the population by herding. Examples of regulations are building code policies which require new properties to be protected against the impacts of extreme weather.

Although requiring individuals to take climate change mitigation and adaptation measures may be viewed as being paternalistic and limiting individual free choice, these requirements may be welfare enhancing if they focus on minimum standards that are cost-effective, such insulation of buildings and elevating properties in flood-prone areas to a minimum height above expected flood water levels. Moreover, financial incentives such as carbon pricing can stimulate consumers and businesses to take measures which save energy and reduce greenhouse gas emissions since high carbon production and consumption would be penalised with a higher price (van den Bergh et al., 2020).

A carbon price would address the common good problem associated with reducing one's carbon footprint since taking individual actions to reduce greenhouse gas emissions results in monetary savings for individuals once carbon is priced. In the absence of carbon pricing these benefits would largely accrue to others in the form of lower climate impacts, resulting in suboptimal incentives for individual action.

In the European Union, higher carbon prices can be achieved by restricting carbon emission permits in the European Emission Trading System, which would increase carbon prices, and by expanding the scope of emissions which fall under this system. Implementing a sufficiently high and stable carbon price would send a strong signal to private investors and firms that low-carbon technologies and production processes will pay off in the long run. High carbon prices also limit the myopia bias in energy conservation because they result in short-term savings on energy bills when households invest in energy-efficiency improvements.

Similar financial incentives can be given to individuals who implement adaptation measures which limit natural disaster damage by rewarding such behaviour with discounts on insurance premiums (Botzen et al., 2009; Mol et al., 2018). The myopia bias can be further addressed by allowing individuals to spread the sometimes high upfront costs of climate change mitigation or adaptation measures through low-interest loans. Means-tested subsidies can further overcome affordability problems amongst low-income households taking these measures (Kousky & Kunreuther, 2014).

2.5   Conclusion

Drastic reductions in greenhouse gas emissions are needed around the world if governments aim to meet the climate policy objectives agreed upon in the Paris Agreement. Moreover, some degree of global warming will inevitably occur and cause impacts on a broad variety of economic sectors and on households, such as increasing losses from natural disasters. The systemic changes required to move to a low-carbon economy, as well as the heterogeneity of adaptation measures needed to limit impacts of climate change, imply that climate action is needed from a wide variety of actors, including governments, firms, and individuals.

Individual perceptions of climate change-related risks are an important driver of both support for climate policy by the public sector and individual decision making about implementing mitigation or adaptation measures. However, individual perceptions of low-probability/high-consequence (LP/HC) risks, such as those associated with climate change, are likely to deviate from expert assessments. Moreover, individual behaviour with regard to LP/HC risks has been associated with a variety of biases and heuristics.

This chapter has reviewed several key factors which shape individual perceptions of climate change risks and discussed the main behavioural biases which hamper individual action. Individual perceptions of climate change appear to be largely driven by political ideology, individual values, and cultural aspects. The main behavioural biases which hamper optimal individual responses to climate change include simplification of risk, availability bias due to underestimating risks in the absence of personal experience, finite pool of worry, myopia (focus on near-term risks), and herding behaviour. Understanding individual risk perceptions and behavioural biases can guide the design of policies which work with these perceptions and biases to improve individual climate action.

Finally, I outlined key elements of a package of climate policy measures which combine communication strategies for making people pay attention to climate change risks with regulations and financial incentives to stimulate energy savings, renewable energy use, and adaptation measures. Another element of this broader climate policy package is choice architecture, such as nudges which encourage climate action by working with social norms. These policy proposals can be seen as an extension of moral inclinations of families and firms, such as the stewardship for the natural environment and the climate, by rewarding such pro-environmental behaviour with financial incentives and encouraging others to take action.

Using perspectives from the field of behavioural economics, this chapter has offered suggestions for enabling an upscaling of climate change mitigation and adaptation actions beyond the sub-group of people currently engaged with the issue of global warming. A broader willingness to contribute to solving this problem, based on intrinsic motivations, is urgently needed if policymakers aim to rapidly transit to a low-carbon economy.

References

Bain, P. G., Hornsey, M. J., Bongiorno, R., & Jeffries, C. (2012). Promoting pro-environmental action in climate change deniers. *Nature Climate Change, 2*, 600–603.

Botzen, W. J. W. (2013). *Managing extreme climate change risks through insurance* (p. 432). Cambridge University Press.

Botzen, W. J. W., Aerts, J. C. J. H., & van den Bergh, J. C. J. M. (2009). Willingness of homeowners to mitigate climate risk through insurance. *Ecological Economics, 68*(8–9), 2265–2277.

Botzen, W. J. W., Kunreuther, H., & Michel-Kerjan, E. (2015). Divergence between individual perceptions and objective indicators of tail risks: Evidence from floodplain residents in New York City. *Judgment and Decision making, 10*(4), 365–385.

Botzen, W. J. W., Michel-Kerjan, E., Kunreuther, H., de Moel, H., & Aerts, J. C. J. H. (2016). Political affiliation affects adaptation to climate risks: Evidence from New York City. *Climatic Change, 138*(1), 353–360.

Botzen, W. J. W., Deschenes, O., & Sanders, M. (2019a). The economic impacts of natural disasters: A review of models and empirical studies. *Review of Environmental Economics and Policy, 13*(2), 167–188.

Botzen, W. J. W., Kunreuther, H. C., Czajkowski, J., & de Moel, H. (2019b). Adoption of individual flood damage mitigation measures in New York City: An extension of protection motivation theory. *Risk Analysis, 39*(10), 2143–2159.

Botzen, W. J. W., Duijndam, S., & van Beukering, P. (2021). Lessons for climate policy from behavioral biases towards COVID-19 and climate change risks. *World Development, 137*, 105214.

Bradt, J. (2019). Comparing the effects of behaviorally-informed interventions on flood insurance demand: An experimental analysis of 'boosts' and 'nudges'. *Behavioural Public Policy*, forthcoming. Available at SSRN: https://ssrn.com/abstract=3424279

Bubeck, P., Botzen, W. J. W., Kreibich, H., & Aerts, J. C. J. H. (2012). Long-term development and effectiveness of private flood mitigation measures: An analysis for the German part of the river Rhine. *Natural Hazards and Earth System Sciences, 12*, 3507–3518.

Bubeck, P., Botzen, W. J. W., Kreibich, H., & Aerts, J. C. J. H. (2013). Detailed insights into the influence of flood-coping appraisals on mitigation behaviour. *Global Environmental Change, 23*(5), 1327–1338.

Capstick, S., Whitmarsh, L., Poortinga, W., Pidgeon, N., & Upham, P. (2015). International trends in public perceptions of climate change over the past quarter century. *Wiley Interdisciplinary Reviews: Climate Change, 6*(1), 35–61.

Chaudhry, S. J., Hand, M., & Kunreuther, H. (2020). *Broad bracketing for low probability events*. The Wharton Risk Management and Decision Processes Center, University of Pennsylvania Working Paper.

Duijndam, S., & van Beukering, P. (2020). Understanding public concern about climate change in Europe, 2008–2017: The influence of economic factors and right-wing populism. *Climate Policy, 21*, 1–15.

Feygina, I., Jost, J. T., & Goldsmith, R. E. (2010). System justification, the denial of global warming, and the possibility of system-sanctioned change. *Personality and Social Psychology Bulletin, 36*, 326–338.

Frederiks, E. R., Stenner, K., & Hobman, E. V. (2015). Household energy use: Applying behavioural economics to understand consumer decision-making and behaviour. *Renewable and Sustainable Energy Reviews, 41*, 1385–1394.

Garde-Hansen, J., McEwen, L., Holmes, A., & Jones, O. (2017). Sustainable flood memory: Remembering as resilience. *Memory Studies, 10*(4), 384–405.

Gelino, B. W., & Reed, D. D. (2020). Temporal discounting of tornado shelter-seeking intentions amidst standard and impact-based weather alerts: A crowdsourced experiment. *Journal of Experimental Psychology: Applied, 26*(1), 16–25.

Gillingham, K., & Palmer, K. (2014). Bridging the energy efficiency gap: Policy insights from economic theory and empirical analysis. *Review of Environmental Economics and Policy, 8*(1), 18–38.

Gromet, D. M., Kunreuther, H., & Larrick, R. P. (2013). Political ideology affects energy-efficiency attitudes and choices. *PNAS, 110*(23), 9314–9319.

Heath, Y., & Gifford, R. (2006). Free-market ideology and environmental degradation: The case of belief in global climate change. *Environment and Behavior, 38*, 48–71.

Hornsey, M. J., Harris, E. A., Bain, P. G., & Fielding, K. S. (2016). Meta-analyses of the determinants and outcomes of belief in climate change. *Nature Climate Change, 6*, 622–626.

IPCC. (2012). Managing the risks of extreme events and disasters to advance climate change adaptation. In C. B. Field, V. Barros, T. F. Stocker, D. Qin, D. J. Dokken, K. L. Ebi, M. D. Mastrandrea, K. J. Mach, G.-K. Plattner, S. K. Allen, M. Tignor, & P. M. Midgley (Eds.),

A special report of working groups I and II of the intergovernmental panel on climate change. Cambridge University Press.

IPCC. (2014). *Climate change 2014: Impacts, adaptation, and vulnerability. Contribution of working group II to the fifth assessment report of the intergovernmental panel on climate change.* Cambridge University Press.

IPCC (2018). *Global warming of 1.5°C. An IPCC special report on the impacts of global warming of 1.5°C above pre-industrial levels and related global greenhouse gas emission pathways, in the context of strengthening the global response to the threat of climate change, sustainable development, and efforts to eradicate poverty.* V. Masson-Delmotte, P. Zhai, H.-O. Pörtner, D. Roberts, J. Skea, P. R. Shukla, A. Pirani, W. Moufouma-Okia, C. Péan, R. Pidcock, S. Connors, J. B. R. Matthews, Y. Chen, X. Zhou, M. I. Gomis, E. Lonnoy, T. Maycock, M. Tignor, & T. Waterfield (Eds.). IPCC.

Kahneman, D. (2011). *Thinking fast and slow.* Farrar, Straus and Giroux.

Kellens, W., Terpstra, T., & De Maeyer, P. (2013). Perception and communication of flood risks: A systematic review of empirical research. *Risk Analysis, 33*(1), 24–49.

Kousky, C., & Kunreuther, H. (2014). Addressing affordability in the National Flood Insurance Program. *Journal of Extreme Events, 1*(01), 1450001.

Kunreuther, H. C. (1996). Mitigating disaster losses through insurance. *Journal of Risk and Uncertainty, 12*(2–3), 171–187.

Kunreuther, H. (2018). Improving the national flood insurance program. *Behavioural Public Policy, 5,* 1–15.

Kunreuther, H. C., Novemsky, N., & Kahneman, D. (2001). Making low probabilities useful. *Journal of Risk and Uncertainty, 23*(2), 161–186.

Mauritsen, T., & Pincus, R. (2017). Committed warming inferred from observations. *Nature Climate Change, 7,* 652–655.

Meyer, R., & Kunreuther, H. (2017). *The ostrich paradox: Why we underprepare for disasters.* Wharton Digital Press.

Mol, J. M., Botzen, W. J. W., & Blasch, J. E. (2018). Behavioral motivations for self-insurance under different disaster risk insurance schemes. *Journal of Economic Behavior & Organization, 180,* 967–991.

Mol, J. M., Botzen, W. J. W., Blasch, J., & de Moel, H. (2020). Insights into flood risk misperceptions of homeowners. *Risk Analysis, 40*(7), 1450–1468.

Nordhaus, W. D. (2015). Climate clubs: Overcoming free-riding in international climate policy. *American Economic Review, 105*(4), 1339–1370.

Osberghaus, D. (2017). The effect of flood experience on household mitigation: Evidence from longitudinal and insurance data. *Global Environmental Change, 43,* 126–136.

Pillay, C., & van den Bergh, J. C. J. M. (2016). Human health impacts of climate change as a catalyst for public engagement: Combining medical, economic and behavioural insights. *International Journal of Climate Change Strategies and Management, 8*(5), 1756–8692.

Robinson, P., & Botzen, W. J. W. (2018). The impact of regret and worry on the threshold level of concern for flood insurance demand: Evidence from Dutch homeowners. *Judgment and Decision making, 13*(3), 237–245.

Robinson, P., & Botzen, W. J. W. (2019). Determinants of probability neglect and risk attitudes for disaster risk: An online experimental study of flood insurance demand among homeowners. *Risk Analysis, 39*(11), 2514–2527.

Rogelj, J., den Elzen, M., Höhne, N., Fransen, T., Fekete, H., Winkler, H., Schaeffer, R., Sha, F., Riahi, K., & Meinshausen, M. (2016). Paris agreement climate proposals need a boost to keep warming well below 2°C. *Nature, 534,* 631–639.

Slovic, P. (2000). *The perception of risk.* Earthscan.

Slovic, P., Fischhoff, B., Lichtenstein, S., Corrigan, B., & Combs, B. (1977). Preference for insuring against probable small losses: Insurance implications. *Journal of Risk and Insurance, 44*(2), 237–258.

Tol, R. S. J. (2018). Economic impacts of climate change. *Review of Environmental Economics and Policy, 12*(1), 4–25.

Tversky, A., & Kahneman, D. (1973). Availability: A heuristic for judging frequency and probability. *Cognitive Psychology, 5*, 207–232.

van den Bergh, J. C. J. M., Angelsen, A., Baranzini, A., Botzen, W. J. W., Carattini, S., Drews, S., Dunlop, T., Galbraith, E., Gsottbauer, E., Howarth, R. B., Padilla, E., Roca, J., & Schmidt, R. (2020). A dual-track transition to global carbon pricing. *Climate Policy, 20*(9), 1057–1069.

van Valkengoed, A. M., & Steg, L. (2019). Meta-analyses of factors motivating climate change adaptation behaviour. *Nature Climate Change, 9*, 158–163.

Whitmarsh, L. (2013). Scepticism and uncertainty about climate change: Dimensions, determinants and change over time. *Global Environmental Change, 21*(2), 690–700.

Wouter Botzen is full Professor of Economics of Global Environmental Change at the Utrecht University School of Economics. Moreover, he is Professor of Economics of Climate Change and Natural Disasters, and Head of the Department of Environmental Economics, Institute for Environmental Studies, VU Amsterdam. He is a senior research fellow at the Risk Management and Decision Processes Center at the Wharton School of the University of Pennsylvania. His main research interests are climate change economics with a particular focus on risk, natural disaster insurance, behavioural economics of decision making under risk, and natural disaster risk assessment and management. He has published widely on these themes.

Chapter 3
Determinants of Belief – And Unbelief – In Climate Change

David Leiser and Pascal Wagner-Egger

Abstract Climate change is a most serious challenge. Committing the needed resources requires that a clear majority of citizens approves the appropriate policies, since committing resources necessarily involve a trade-off with other expenses. However, there are distinct groups of people who remain in denial about the realities of climatic change. This chapter presents a range of psychological and social phenomena that together explain the phenomena that lead to denial.

3.1 The Scientific Consensus and Public Reception

There exists a scientific consensus that climate change is real, important, and anthropogenic. This was first shown by Oreskes (2004, 2018), and confirmed by later studies. Anderegg et al. (2010) found that 97% of the climate researchers most actively publishing in the field support the tenets of anthropogenic climate change, as outlined by the Intergovernmental Panel on Climate Change (Their latest report is IPCC, 2014; see also O'Neill et al., 2017).

Most people have come to recognize the fact and many do worry about it. A report by the Pew Research Center (Fagan & Huang, 2019) found that concerns about climate change rose significantly in many countries during the last decade. Majorities in most surveyed countries consider global climate change to be a major threat to their nation. In the US, close to 70% of people surveyed recognize that global warming is taking place, vs only 16% who think this is not the case. While US respondents tend to be less concerned about climate change, 59% still see it as a serious threat. A slim majority also understands that global warming is mostly human-caused (Leiserowitz et al., 2019). Moreover, about half of Americans (53%)

D. Leiser
Department of Psychology, Ben Gurion University, Beersheba, Israel
e-mail: dleiser@bgu.ac.il

P. Wagner-Egger (✉)
Université de Fribourg, Fribourg, Switzerland
e-mail: pascal.wagner@unifr.ch

© The Author(s) 2022
A. Siegmann (ed.), *Climate of the Middle*, SpringerBriefs in Climate Studies,
https://doi.org/10.1007/978-3-030-85322-8_3

know that scientists concur that global warming is happening. In France (IFOP, 2018), 67% of a representative survey agree that climate change is a problem mainly caused by human activity, but 24% think that it is not clear whether global warming is due to human activity or to solar radiation, while 6% thinks that global warming is not certain, and 3% consider that global warming is a hoax.

While there is now a "consensus on there being a consensus" amongst scientists about the reality of climate change, as Cook et al. (2018) put it, significant parts of the public are less certain about it. Several factors determine the extent of belief in climate change: motivational, cognitive (Rutjens et al., 2018) and socio-political. These factors, which we will discuss in turn in this chapter, interact with one another, and culminate in conspirational ideation. In a recent meta-analysis, Hornsey et al. (2016) observed that values, ideologies, worldviews and political orientation had more explanatory power about climate change beliefs than education, gender, subjective knowledge, and experience of extreme weather events.

3.2 Cognitive, Motivational and Social Determinants of Disbelief in Climate Change

It is often believed that reasoning consists of a set of cognitive processes—strategies for accessing, constructing, and evaluating beliefs – intended to reach a true conclusion. But motivated reasoning (Kunda, 1990) is a powerful force, that thwarts this goal. An individual's motivations affect their cognitive processes of reasoning and judgment. Rejection of science should be seen in this context: when its conclusions are unpalatable to an individual, they may resort to distortions of the normative reasoning processes (Lewandowsky et al., 2018; Lewandowsky & Oberauer, 2016).

Confirmation bias is one such cognitive and motivational distortion, which involves greater scrutiny and counter-argumentation of information contrary to one's prior belief compared to information that supports it (Nickerson, 1998), along with greater motivation to confirm than to disconfirm one's beliefs (Anderson et al., 1980). This can take the comparatively benign form of willful ignorance, as illustrated by an ethnographic study by Norgaard (2006) in a wealthy rural Norwegian community. Because Norwegian economic prosperity is tied to oil production in the North Sea, collectively ignoring climate change maintains Norwegians' economic interests. Accordingly, many of them "don't really want to know" about climate change and dismiss inconvenient facts (though this attitude did not deter the Norwegian government from imposing a carbon tax). The reliance on apparent disconfirmations of global warming, such as the local occurrence of unusual cold episodes, as was famously illustrated by Donald Trump would be another illustration[1].

---

[1] https://www.cnbc.com/2017/12/29/trump-revives-misleading-claim-its-cold-so-global-warming-isnt-real.html

Motivated Reasoning

At least two determinants of motivated reasoning about climate change denial may be postulated. One is a general distrust of authorities, as we will discuss below, the other is *cognitive dissonance* (Festinger, 1957), defined as the motivation to decrease contradiction between two cognitive elements. In our case, as people dislike changing their habits about consumption, travels, food, etc. (Gardner & Rebar, 2019) climate change challenges our existing behaviors. This gives rise to cognitive dissonance, as a change in behaviors is required, leading to motivated reasoning to reduce the dissonance.

In addition to confirmation bias, information and misinformation have become readily accessible with the advent of the internet. This results in an increase of confirmation bias because internet's algorithms confine people in echo chambers, which presents people with congenial information (Bronner, 2015; Pariser, 2011). Another consequence is the decrease in epistemic deference towards specialists (Anderegg et al., 2010; Kahan, 2012; Kahan et al., 2011a, b; Nichols, 2014). This socio-political factor is one of the reasons for the rise of conspiracy theories (Douglas et al., 2019). Trust in scientists and in science is decreasing. In the US, among Conservatives (but not Liberals) trust in science has been declining since the 1970s (Gauchat, 2012). Climate science has become particularly polarized, with Conservatives being more likely than Liberals to reject the notion that greenhouse gas emissions are warming the globe (Lewandowsky et al., 2013a). While the drop in the trust in science is more marked in the US than elsewhere (Hornsey et al., 2018), it may be found in other countries as well, (see the situation in France, IFOP representative survey, 2018).

Motivated reasoning can lead people holding strong views to question the credentials of specialists who hold views opposed to their own (Hart & Nisbet, 2012; Kahan et al., 2011a, b). For example, Kahan et al. (2011a, b) invented academic authorities whose made-up CV presented an impressive academic and occupational profile. Their study manipulated the views ascribed to those authorities on various controversial issues (such as climate change or gun control) in which they were supposedly top-notch specialist. It was found that when the views attributed to the specialists contradicted those of the respondent, their expertise was judged questionable. This explains why more information about there being a consensus about climate change does not necessarily increase belief about the consensus.

While for most people (Cook & Lewandowsky, 2016) such information results, as it should, in a stronger belief, the opposite was true for people for whom this information is very unwelcome. For the more extremely ideological people (as measured in the extent of their support for the free market economic model), more information about the scientific consensus weakened their belief in an existing consensus. Simply put, people are willing to trust real experts, but may reserve the right to identify real experts according to whether their views are congenial or not. In such cases, the competency of the experts is impugned.

3.3   Conspiratorial Thinking

To avoid accepting an unpalatable conclusion, some people may judge that the scientists who hold that view should be dismissed as untrustworthy. To them, if those scientists profess that view, it is not because they studied the evidence and reached the same conclusion according to the accepted canons of the scientific method. Rather, they profess that view because they are engaged in a secretive conspiracy (Diethelm & McKee, 2009).

This alternative (my opponent is either incompetent or a knave) sometimes leads climate science denialists to harass researchers critical of their views (Lewandowsky, 2019). Less dramatically, one of us debated about and ran endless supplemental statistical analyses during 1 week in an effort to argue with a denialist who was strenuously looking for errors in our data analysis (Wagner-Egger et al., 2018).

Distrust toward experts and official views as a product of confirmation bias is typical of "conspiracy theories" (CT), and indeed renders such beliefs resistant to disconfirmation: if anyone who argues against a belief is considered as being incompetent or a deliberate liar, that belief is effectively shielded by epistemic closure. (McHoskey, 1995) submitted equal-sized long texts to his participants, one endorsing the conspiracist explanation of J.F. Kennedy's assassination in 1963, one in favor of the official version (lone gunner). The endorsement of the CT about Kennedy's death was also measured for each participant, allowing to compare a group of believers and a group of nonbelievers in the CTs. Results showed that both believers and nonbelievers committed biased assimilation of the information given, and judged the information in line with their preexisting beliefs as more convincing than the rival information, and to an extent proportional to the extremeness of their preexisting attitude. But the CTs believers increased their belief in the CT after having read both texts, indicating a more potent confirmation bias among them.

As we mentioned above, CTs are related to distrust of political, judicial and journalistic authorities (e.g., Douglas et al., 2019). It is therefore unsurprising that the distrust is also directed toward science and experts. CTs have been observed about epidemics (e.g., AIDS, (Herek & Capitanio, 1994); swine flu, (Wagner-Egger et al., 2011); coronavirus pandemic (Oleksy et al., 2020), GMOs, vaccines, etc.. Some people are more prone than others to display this conspiratorial way of reasoning (Uscinski et al., 2017; Uscinski & Olivella, 2017), and belief in diverse CTs tends to correlate. Socio-political, psychological and cognitive factors have been found to correlate with (and sometimes cause) beliefs in CTs. Extreme political positions (and more at the right than at the left extreme), lower social status, minority belonging, paranoid and anxious feelings, and irrational beliefs (paranormal beliefs, intuitive thinking, cognitive biases, fake news sensitivity, etc.) are positively correlated with CTs adhesion in dozens of studies.

The Perception of Climate Science as a Conspiracy

Conspiracists beliefs predict a rejection of climate science. Lewandowski and colleagues (Lewandowsky et al., 2013a, b) observed in a sample of climate blog users and a representative US sample that conspiracist beliefs (for example that the FBI killed Martin Luther King, or that MI6 assassinated Princess Diana) were related to climate skepticism and other scientific realities (that HIV causes AIDS, smoking causes lung cancer; opposition to GMOs and to vaccines). This correlation is found in Europe too. In a IFOP representative survey in France in 2018, a significant correlation between CTs beliefs (about Apollo mission, chemtrails, etc.) and rejection of climate science has also been observed (IFOP, 2018). In another US representative sample, Uscinski & Olivella (2017) found that conspiracy thinking and political partisanship (political right) predicted climate denialism.

Other studies showed not only a correlational but also a causal link between CTs beliefs and climate change skepticism. (Van der Linden, 2015) randomly assigned participants to three experimental conditions, and had them watch a short video that presented either a climate change conspiracy video, or one that argued for the existence of climate change, or a neutral video on an unrelated topic. Following exposure to the climate conspiracy video, individuals updated their beliefs in line with the conspiracy information, making respondents less likely to believe in the existence of scientific consensus on human-induced climate change, and also less likely to sign a petition aimed at reducing global warming, compared to the other groups.

This association between conspiracist ideation and anti-science feelings may have serious negative social consequences in many domains. When holding CTs about epidemics or vaccines, people will display more risky behavior, such as not using condoms (Bogart & Bird, 2003; Bogart & Thorburn, 2005) or refusing to have their children vaccinated (Jolley & Douglas, 2014a). And of course, CTs about climate change decreases ecological intentions to reduce one's carbon footprint (Jolley & Douglas, 2014b).

Sadly, scientists are not immune to motivated reasoning. This manifests itself in the prior attitude effect, where the perceived strength of novel information depends on the pre-existing belief. People who had the benefit of scientific training are in a better position to find facts that support their beliefs and reasons to reject whatever information is opposed to them. They can deploy a confirmation bias, and seek out information that confirms their prior belief, but are also adept at finding faults in research that would contradict their views. And indeed, individuals with greater science literacy and scientific training tend to have more polarized beliefs about controversial science topics (Drummond & Fischhoff, 2017). In particular, Kahan et al. observed that increased science literacy and numeracy led people to more polarized views about climate change (Braman et al., 2005; Kahan, 2012; Kahan et al., 2012; West et al., 2012).

3.4   Doubt and Uncertainty as a Political Strategy

Absent a proper understanding of complex issues, people often accept as true whatever is believed by people in their environment and presented to them by opinion leaders. In the US, belief in anthropogenic climate change has become a partisan issue, with conservatives being skeptical or dismissive about it, leading to more extensive rejection of the scientific consensus about climate change. The partisan gap is extensive, both about the reality of climate change (Fagan & Huang, 2019) and about the extent of the consensus amongst scientists about it, with conservatives underestimating it more than liberals (Cook & Lewandowsky, 2016). This gap is more marked in the US than in other countries (Chinn et al., 2020; Druckman & McGrath, 2019; Goldberg et al., 2020; Karakas & Mitra, 2020).

To understand the origin of this disparity, some historical background is needed. In the eighties, the fossil fuel industry correctly identified that the use of their products could lead to climate warming via the greenhouse effect (Banerjee et al., 2015). Energy companies set up several organizations, such as the Global Climate Coalition, the American Petroleum Institute and the Information Council for the Environment, to fund vast campaigns designed to influence public opinion. These campaigns lead to the polarization observed today (Dunlap & McCright, 2011).

The overall strategy consisted in promoting skepticism by conservative think-tanks funded by the fossil fuel industry (Hall, 2015). Skepticism is the operative term here. The campaign was not intended to convince people that there is no climate change, but to make them doubt, or in the famous phrase (Information Council for the Environment, 1991): "reposition global warming as theory, not fact." That campaign was exposed in various publications (Climate Investigation Center, September 29, 2020).

Doubt and uncertainty were sufficient for their purpose, since near-certainty must be achieved to promote far-reaching economic and technological changes. Moreover, it is very difficult to argue against doubt. Controversy is usually taken as involving two opposing positions, amongst which people try to arbitrate by looking at the evidence. As we saw, people resist a change of opinion, using disconfirmation bias and selective search for information. That resistance will eventually break down in the face of overwhelming evidence, bringing about a conversion. But there is a third position, much harder to challenge, namely the agnostic one. Inasmuch as there is no pre-determined point where everyone must concede that something has been proven, people may reserve judgment indefinitely. The agnostic position is therefore more or less immune to the effect studied by Festinger, allowing its proponents to claim the mantle of fair, impartial and prudent judgment ad infinitum.

3.5   Conclusion

Climate change is a most serious challenge. Committing the needed resources requires that a clear majority of citizens approves the appropriate policies, since committing resources necessarily involve a trade-off with other expenses. This chapter presented a range of psychological and social phenomena that jointly explain the difficulty in meeting the challenge. Reasoning is often distorted by motivations, including the motivation to not be proven wrong. This can lead to a will to disqualify the scientific bearers of inconvenient truths. In its more extreme form, this tendency can develop into conspiratorial thinking, especially in a context of diminished trust in expertise and in political elites. Finally, these tendencies may be reinforced by vested interests, whose tactics on the issue of climate change has involved sowing uncertainty to produce political immobilism.

References

Anderegg, W. R. L., Prall, J. W., Harold, J., & Schneider, S. H. (2010). Expert credibility in climate change. *Proceedings of the National Academy of Sciences, 107*(27), 12107–12109.

Anderson, C. A., Lepper, M. R., & Ross, L. (1980). Perseverance of social theories : The role of explanation in the persistence of discredited information. *Journal of Personality and Social Psychology, 39*(6), 1037–1049. https://doi.org/10.1037/h0077720

Banerjee, N., Song, L., & Hasemyer, D. (2015). *Exxon: The road not taken*. Retrieved from https://insideclimatenews.org/content/Exxon-The-Road-Not-Taken

Bogart, L. M., & Bird, S. T. (2003). Exploring the relationship of conspiracy beliefs about HIV/AIDS to sexual behaviors and attitudes among African-American adults. *Journal of the National Medical Association, 95*(11), 1057.

Bogart, L. M., & Thorburn, S. (2005). Are HIV/AIDS conspiracy beliefs a barrier to HIV prevention among African Americans? *JAIDS Journal of Acquired Immune Deficiency Syndromes, 38*(2), 213–218.

Braman, D., Kahan, D., & Grimmelmann, J. (2005). Modeling facts, culture, and cognition in the gun debate. *Social Justice Research, 18*(3), 283–304.

Bronner, G. (2015). *Belief and misbelief asymmetry on the internet*. Wiley.

Chinn, S., Hart, P. S., & Soroka, S. (2020). Politicization and polarization in climate change news content, 1985-2017. *Science Communication, 42*(1), 112–129.

Climate Investigation Center. (2020, September 29). *Climatefiles – Hard to find documents all in one place*. Retrieved from www.climatefiles.com

Cook, J., & Lewandowsky, S. (2016). Rational irrationality: Modeling climate change belief polarization using Bayesian networks. *Topics in Cognitive Science, 8*(1), 160–179.

Cook, J., van der Linden, S., Maibach, E., & Lewandowsky, S. (2018). The consensus handbook.

Diethelm, P., & McKee, M. (2009). Denialism: What is it and how should scientists respond? *The European Journal of Public Health, 19*(1), 2–4.

Douglas, K. M., Uscinski, J. E., Sutton, R. M., Cichocka, A., Nefes, T., Ang, C. S., & Deravi, F. (2019). Understanding conspiracy theories. *Political Psychology, 40*(S1), 3–35.

Druckman, J. N., & McGrath, M. C. (2019). The evidence for motivated reasoning in climate change preference formation. *Nature Climate Change, 9*(2), 111–119.

Drummond, C., & Fischhoff, B. (2017). Individuals with greater science literacy and education have more polarized beliefs on controversial science topics. *Proceedings of the National Academy of Sciences, 114*(36), 9587–9592.

Dunlap, R. E., & McCright, A. M. (2011). Organized climate change denial. In *The Oxford handbook of climate change and society* (Vol. 1, pp. 144–160). Oxford University Press.

Fagan, M., & Huang, C. (2019, April). A look at how people around the world view climate chang. *Factank – News in the numbers*. Retrieved from https://www.pewresearch.org/fact-tank/2019/04/18/a-look-at-how-people-around-the-world-view-climate-change/

Festinger, L. (1957). *A theory of cognitive dissonance* (Vol. 2). Stanford University Press.

Gardner, B., & Rebar, A. L. (2019). Habit formation and behavior change. In *Oxford research encyclopedia of psychology*. Oxford University Press.

Gauchat, G. (2012). Politicization of science in the public sphere: A study of public Trust in the United States, 1974 to 2010. *American Sociological Review, 77*(2), 167–187.

Goldberg, M. H., Gustafson, A., Ballew, M. T., Rosenthal, S. A., & Leiserowitz, A. (2020). Identifying the most important predictors of support for climate policy in the United States. *Behavioural Public Policy, 5*, 1–23.

Hall, S. (2015). Exxon Knew about Climate Change almost 40 years ago. *Scientific American, Online October 26,* https://www.scientificamerican.com/article/exxon-knew-about-climate-change-almost-40-years-ago/ Retrieved 19 June 2021.

Hart, P. S., & Nisbet, E. C. (2012). Boomerang effects in science communication: How motivated reasoning and identity cues amplify opinion polarization about climate mitigation policies. *Communication Research, 39*(6), 701–723.

Herek, G. M., & Capitanio, J. P. (1994). Conspiracies, contagion, and compassion: Trust and public reactions to AIDS. *AIDS Education and Prevention, 6*, 365–375.

Hornsey, M. J., Harris, E. A., Bain, P. G., & Fielding, K. S. (2016). Meta-analyses of the determinants and outcomes of belief in climate change. *Nature Climate Change, 6*, 622–626.

Hornsey, M. J., Harris, E. A., & Fielding, K. S. (2018). Relationships among conspiratorial beliefs, conservatism and climate scepticism across nations. *Nature Clim Change, 8*, 614–620.

Information Council for the Environment. (1991). *Mission statement – Strategies; reposition warming as theory (Not Fact).* In. American Meteorological Society Archives.

IFOP. (2018). *Enquête sur le complotisme, ConspiracyWatch and Foundation Jean Jaurès.* Available at: https://jean-jaures.org/sites/default/files/redac/commun/productions/2018/0108/115158_-_rapport_02.01.2017.pdf. Accessed 22 Aug 2019.

IPCC. (2014). *Climate change 2014: Synthesis report. Contribution of working groups I, II and III to the fifth assessment report of the intergovernmental panel on climate change.* Retrieved from https://www.ipcc.ch/report/ar5/syr/

Jolley, D., & Douglas, K. M. (2014a). The effects of anti-vaccine conspiracy theories on vaccination intentions. *PLoS One, 9*(2), e89177.

Jolley, D., & Douglas, K. M. (2014b). The social consequences of conspiracism: Exposure to conspiracy theories decreases intentions to engage in politics and to reduce one's carbon footprint. *British Journal of Psychology, 105*(1), 35–56.

Kahan, D. M. (2012). Ideology, motivated reasoning, and cognitive reflection: An experimental study. *SSRN Electronic Journal, 8*(4), 407–424.

Kahan, D. M., Jenkins-Smith, H., & Braman, D. (2011a). Cultural cognition of scientific consensus. *Journal of Risk Research, 14*(2), 147–174.

Kahan, D. M., Wittlin, M., Peters, E., Slovic, P., Ouellette, L. L., Braman, D., & Mandel, G. N. (2011b). *The tragedy of the risk-perception commons: culture conflict, rationality conflict, and climate change.* Temple University legal studies research paper (2011–26).

Kahan, D. M., Peters, E., Wittlin, M., Slovic, P., Ouellette, L. L., Braman, D., & Mandel, G. (2012). The polarizing impact of science literacy and numeracy on perceived climate change risks. *Nature Climate Change, 2*(10), 732–735.

Karakas, L. D., & Mitra, D. (2020). Believers vs. deniers: Climate change and environmental policy polarization. *European Journal of Political Economy, 65*, 101948.

Kunda, Z. (1990). The case for motivated reasoning. *Psychological Bulletin, 108*(3), 480.

Leiserowitz, A., Maibach, E. W., Rosenthal, S., Kotcher, J., Bergquist, P., Ballew, M., … Gustafson, A. (2019). *Climate change in the American mind: April 2019. Yale University and George Mason University.* Yale Program on Climate Change Communication.

Lewandowsky, S. (2019). In whose hands the future. In S. Lewandowsky & J. E. Uscinski (Eds.), *Conspiracy theories and the people who believe them* (pp. 149–177). Oxford University Press.

Lewandowsky, S., & Oberauer, K. (2016). Motivated rejection of science. *Current Directions in Psychological Science, 25*(4), 217–222.

Lewandowsky, S., Gignac, G. E., & Oberauer, K. (2013a). The role of conspiracist ideation and worldviews in predicting rejection of science. *PLoS One, 8*(10), e75637.

Lewandowsky, S., Oberauer, K., & Gignac, G. E. (2013b). NASA faked the moon landing—Therefore,(climate) science is a hoax an anatomy of the motivated rejection of science. *Psychological Science, 24*(5), 622–633.

Lewandowsky, S., Cook, J., & Lloyd, E. (2018). The 'Alice in Wonderland' mechanics of the rejection of (climate) science: Simulating coherence by conspiracism. *Synthese, 195*(1), 175–196.

McHoskey, J. W. (1995). Case closed? On the John F. Kennedy assassination: Biased assimilation of evidence and attitude polarization. *Basic and Applied Social Psychology, 17*(3), 395–409.

Nichols, T. (2014). *The death of expertise: The Campaign against established knowledge and why it matters.* Retrieved from http://thefederalist.com/2014/01/17/the-death-of-expertise/

Nickerson, R. S. (1998). Confirmation Bias: A Ubiquitous Phenomenon in Many Guises. *Review of GeneralPsychology, 2*(2), 175–220.

Norgaard, K. M. (2006). "We don't really want to know" – Environmental justice and socially organized denial of global warming in Norway. *Organization & Environment, 19*(3), 347–370.

O'Neill, B. C., Oppenheimer, M., Warren, R., Hallegatte, S., Kopp, R. E., Pörtner, H. O., … Yohe, G. (2017). IPCC reasons for concern regarding climate change risks. *Nature Climate Change, 7*(1), 28–37.

Oleksy, T., Wnuk, A., Maison, D., & Łyś, A. (2020). Content matters. Different predictors and social consequences of general and government-related conspiracy theories on COVID-19. *Personality and Individual Differences, 168*, 110289.

Oreskes, N. (2004). Beyond the ivory tower. The scientific consensus on climate change. *Science, 306*(5702), 1686.

Oreskes, N. (2018). The scientific consensus on climate change: How do we know we're not wrong? In *Climate modelling* (pp. 31–64). Springer.

Pariser, E. (2011). *The filter bubble: What the internet is hiding from you.* Penguin UK.

Rutjens, B. T., Heine, S. J., Sutton, R. M., & van Harreveld, F. (2018). Attitudes towards science. In *Advances in experimental social psychology* (Vol. 57, pp. 125–165). Elsevier.

Uscinski, J. E., & Olivella, S. (2017). The conditional effect of conspiracy thinking on attitudes toward climate change. *Research & Politics, 4*(4), 2053168017743105.

Uscinski, J. E., Douglas, K., & Lewandowsky, S. (2017). Climate change conspiracy theories. In *Oxford research encyclopedia of climate science.* Oxford University Press.

Van der Linden, S. (2015). The conspiracy-effect: Exposure to conspiracy theories (about global warming) decreases pro-social behavior and science acceptance. *Personality and Individual Differences, 87*, 171–173.

Wagner-Egger, P., Bangerter, A., Gilles, I., Green, E., Rigaud, D., Krings, F., … Clémence, A. (2011). Lay perceptions of collectives at the outbreak of the H1N1 epidemic: Heroes, villains and victims. *Public Understanding of Science, 20*(4), 461–476.

Wagner-Egger, P., Delouvée, S., Gauvrit, N., & Dieguez, S. (2018). Creationism and conspiracism share a common teleological bias. *Current Biology, 28*(16), R867–R868.

West, R. F., Meserve, R. J., & Stanovich, K. E. (2012). Cognitive sophistication does not attenuate the bias blind spot. *Journal of Personality and Social Psychology, 103*(3), 506.

David Leiser is professor of psychology at Ben-Gurion University of the Negev, specializing in Economic psychology and Social psychology. Leiser has served as President of the Economic Psychology division of the International Association of Applied Psychology (IAAP) since 2014. His main focus is on economic psychology, with an emphasis on investigating how lay people understand economic issues and phenomena, both in micro– and macro-economics. He wrote 'How We Misunderstand Economics And Why It Matters: The Psychology of Bias, Distortion and Conspiracy', with Yhonatan Shemesh (Routledge, 2018). David was president of the International Association for Research in Economic Psychology (IAREP) in 2011–2014.

Pascal Wagner-Egger is Lecturer at the Department of Psychology of the University of Fribourg (Switzerland) and co-director of the Unit of Psycholinguistics and Applied Social Psychology. His research focuses on beliefs, reasoning, racism/sexism and social representations.

Chapter 4
Climate Catastrophes as a Sum of Known Risks

Francisco Estrada

Abstract An ever-increasing body of research has warned for decades about the impacts of climate change on agriculture, health, flooding, economy, among many others and provided information about when and where these impacts could be larger. Are societies prepared for these expected 'white-swans', particularly in the context of a high degree of interconnectedness in Nature and in society? I borrow from the development of the Covid-19 pandemic to illustrate this view. Influenza pandemics have been foreseen decades before, but the characteristics of the virus and the socioeconomic links have made it into the global crisis that it had become in 2020.

4.1 Introduction

The Covid-19 pandemic immediate message is that all countries are much more vulnerable to white-swan type of events and at much higher risk than previously thought. While initially a problem and its consequences may be foreseeable, the properties and interactions of complex natural and human systems can transform, amplify and transmit shocks in unexpected and unpredictable ways. Unpredictable events with major consequences, known as black swans, —or at least long, dark shadows from white swans— can arise as the outcome of otherwise predictable, manageable events.

This holds a lesson for the problem of climate change, which is one of the systemic socioenvironmental challenges that will pose more complex, uncertain and highly correlated problems in this century. The literature strongly suggests not only predictable impacts across natural and human systems, but the existence of ontological uncertainty and the possibility of surprises. The current pandemic should help to better gauge how confident one should be about current estimates of the magnitude of the impacts of global socioenvironmental issues.

F. Estrada (✉)
Universidad Nacional Autónoma de México & Vrije Universiteit,
Amsterdam, The Netherlands
e-mail: feporrua@atmosfera.unam.mx

© The Author(s) 2022
A. Siegmann (ed.), *Climate of the Middle*, SpringerBriefs in Climate Studies,
https://doi.org/10.1007/978-3-030-85322-8_4

4.2   Difficulties in Grasping the Scale and Impact
of the Problem

For much of the media, decision-makers and the general public, it is difficult to grapple with the climate problem. And, as argued here, there are good reasons for that. Climate change is a "wicked" problem that does not easily lends itself to be simplified in such a way that becomes easy to understand, communicate, much less to create policy for and to implement practical strategies to tackle it. It is a systemic problem and thus there is no simple way to characterize what its boundaries are; it is a long-memory problem for which current actions have considerable bearing in temporal scales we suffer from strong cognitive biases; it is riddled with epistemic uncertainty blurring our view not only of distant horizons, but the present and even the past in terms of data, knowledge about physics of climate and relevant aspects of the systems being affected by it, such as their sensitivity, coping and adaptation capacities. These difficulties can foster a wide range of contrasting beliefs and narratives that can lead to divergent perceptions of risk that polarize society and policymakers alike about climate policy. However, a good part of the basic ideas behind these opposing narratives share, without realizing it, similar biases.

Significant changes in global climate occur on timescales of centuries. However, while some physical aspects of climate change are "slow", such as the accumulation of greenhouse gases in the atmosphere, sea level rise and the warming of the deep oceans, this is not true for all physical aspects of climate change, nor for all spatial scales or the variety of impacts occurring over natural and human systems. Some estimates suggest that, at the global scale, the impacts of climate change during the last decades of the twentieth century became comparable in magnitude to those of natural climate variability (Estrada et al., 2017b). Damages from climate change are a function of changes in hazard, but also of a diversity of factors determining vulnerability, coping and adaptation capacities (Estrada et al., 2019; Field et al., 2012). All these are highly heterogeneous across and within regions and societies, and characterizing climate change as a "slow" problem to be worried about only in the far future may not be accurate for a significant part of the world's population (Adler et al., 2017; Ignjacevic et al., 2020; Ricke et al., 2018; Tol, 2009). Moreover, this view fails to accurately reflect the current understanding about trends in some extreme events (Field et al., 2012; Stott, 2016), as well as the existence of evidence but lack of consensus in some others, such as changes in economic damages from hurricanes and tropical storms (Botzen et al., 2020; Estrada et al., 2015b; Grinsted et al., 2019; Nordhaus, 2010), and the limited information we have about probabilities and thresholds that may trigger climate catastrophes (Cheng et al., 2013).

The ratification of the Paris Agreement by the vast majority of countries shows the existence of a consensus about the seriousness of the climate change problem and the need to reduce the associated risks (Lawrence & Schäfer, 2019;

Schellnhuber et al., 2016). Large uncertainties exist about the political willingness, feasibility and costs for the required stringent mitigation actions (Cox et al., 2018; Millar et al., 2017; Rogelj et al., 2018). The lack of results from international climate policy during the past 30 years suggests that while in the political discourse climate change occupies a high priority, the urgency has not permeated into the realm of actions so much. The current state of global climate policy can justifiably foster pessimistic expectations about the future. This view has the realism of the catastrophic impacts climate change and political paralysis can bring, but could underestimate the mechanisms of the civil society to bring political change, rapid shifts in technological trends and economic opportunities for a cleaner and more sustainable development (Zhenmin & Espinosa, 2019), as well as the abilities of natural and human systems to deal with change and challenges. Technology and education can help coping with, and adapting to, some of the foreseeable consequences of climate change (Anthoff & Tol, 2012; Haer et al., 2018; Tol et al., 2007). However, as argued below, probably the main risk comes from the interactions of concurrent problems that in the context of complex systems can overcome our capacities to cope and adapt and lead to potential catastrophes.

The opinion on the ontology of the climate change problem is not just an academic problem. The way we see the world influences how we choose to deal with it. In such a politically polarized world we live in nowadays, this can end up in some circles as a cartoonish conundrum: on the one hand, if the climate problem is slow-moving and non-catastrophic, societies do not need to adapt quickly and CO_2-emissions do not have to be brought down that fast. It may even be thought that cleaner production and emission standards can be postponed for decades. On the other hand, if catastrophic events are just around the corner, we should stop doing what we are doing and put the reduction of greenhouse gases above all other priorities that we might have. These differences are frequently debated but the other part of the equation defining climate change consequences is often forgotten: how well are societies prepared to deal with the catastrophic and non-catastrophic risks and impacts?

There are fundamental differences between climate change and pandemic risks but also striking similarities regarding its causes, consequences and the behavioral biases societies suffer (Botzen et al., 2021). Pandemics are experienced as discrete acute events, climate change is commonly conceived as a long-term, chronic problem that gets worse over time and that is accompanied by acute, discrete events, such as extreme realizations of weather and climate (Field et al., 2012; Hoegh-Guldberg et al., 2018). These problems are not independent as they share common drivers: anthropogenic perturbation of natural systems seem to be imposing an accelerating trend to the emergence and reemergence of infectious diseases and increase their transmission (Brooks & Boeger, 2019; Morens & Fauci, 2020; Watts et al., 2020). Despite their differences, we can learn valuable lessons from Covid-19 about our response to global challenges such as climate change.

4.3   The Apparent Predictability and Manageability of Climate Change

The consequences of climate change on natural and human systems have been studied for more than 40 years, and although the existence of ontological uncertainty (unknown unknowns) and the possibility of surprises are recognized, governments and societies treat this as problem that can be handled within the boundaries of standard approaches and methods, timeframes and relatively small additional efforts. A considerable portion of the peer-reviewed estimates suggest this phenomenon may have a modest impact on the world's economy and thus stringent mitigation actions are not justified (Mendelsohn, 2010; Tol, 2009).

While accounting for the possibility of climate catastrophes, nonlinearities and tipping points has shown these estimates to rise, they seem not to tilt the balance enough for triggering significantly larger mitigation efforts (Anthoff et al., 2016; Colt & Knapp, 2016; Mendelsohn et al., 2016; Nordhaus, 2011; Weitzman, 2009). Ethical and distributional concerns between and within regions, long-run consequences and modelling limitations have also been brought forward as reasons to support higher levels of concern and action (Estrada et al., 2015a; Stern, 2013; Tol, 2018). However, leading economic models suggest allowing an increase of 3.5 °C in global temperatures at the end of this century could be the optimal climate policy (Nordhaus, 2018). It is worth noting that such estimate accounts for the possibility of occurrence of climate catastrophes. However, an increasing body of evidence suggests that the results of existing economic models may reveal more about the limitations of current research methods and oversimplified systems' representations, than of the severity of climate change consequences (Botzen et al., 2020; Estrada et al., 2015a, 2017a; Stern, 2013; Van den Bergh & Botzen, 2014; Van den Bergh & Botzen, 2015).

4.4   The Corona Crisis as a Harbinger of Climate Risks

Because of the high connectivity of the modern world, the current Covid-19 pandemic was not only foreseeable but expected (Contini et al., 2020; Scarpino & Petri, 2019). Scientists have warned for influenza pandemics before, and earlier virus outbreaks such as SARS and Swine flu have shown that local outbreaks of a novel virus can quickly spread globally. The interconnection of the modern world is made possible by airplanes and global shipping. The means of global transportation facilitate trade, the exchange of ideas and tourism, but also the spreading of diseases.

Because we were warned, the Covid-19 pandemic cannot be considered as a 'Black Swan' type of event. These events are defined by three main conditions: (1) being outside the realm of regular expectation and probability theory, (2) they produce impacts of historic proportions and; (3) in retrospect they seem predictable and explainable and thus their unpredictable nature is incorrectly dismissed

(Aven, 2013; Taleb, 2007). Although, given the observed outcomes in terms of health and socioeconomic impacts, this event is of historic proportions, current scientific knowledge and historic data indicates that this pandemic violates the first and third conditions. A vast amount of scientific literature warned about the occurrence of pandemic events (Cheng et al., 2007; Fan et al., 2018; Hill et al., 2017; Poland et al., 2007), to the extent such events have even been absorbed by pop-culture for decades. However, its global impact has been much larger than expected, changing how people live, including their social interactions and the economy. These effects are projected to be highly persistent and, in some cases, even permanent, leading to the perception that the world has to transit to a "new normality" in which some aspects in the post-pandemic life could be fundamentally different in commerce, tourism, mobility and a wide range of social interactions (De Vos, 2020).

At the time of writing this text, globally more than 65 million people have been confirmed as infected, more than 1.5 million people have died from Covid-19, health systems in most countries have faced severe challenges to manage the emergency, there have been considerable shortages of medical supplies and equipment, and a significant share of the world's population is under lockdown or quarantine, pushing the economy to an unparalleled standstill. The resulting socioeconomic impacts are expected to be unprecedented in recent history and their long-run effects are unknown.

Covid-19 illustrates that socioenvironmental problems do not present themselves in isolation. Its effects have been painfully amplified by underlying systemic socio-economic and environmental issues, such as the fragile state of health systems, the inadequacy of governmental measures for prevention and control, poverty and inequality, environmental degradation, air quality among many more. This initially foreseeable problem for which we should have been prepared for, was transformed into a much less predictable, manageable and containable situation that involves unknow consequences and derivations in the political, social and economic realms at the local, regional and global scales. Learning from this experience is of outmost importance for facing the global socioenvironmental problems that we know will endure this century. One of these challenges is global warming.

4.5 Catastrophes as Cascades of Foreseeable Problems

Climate change represents a much more complicated problem since it is expected to affect a wide range of aspects of human and natural systems simultaneously, and thus creating highly correlated risks that will be very hard to manage or hedge against. The compound risk of climate change and of other environmental and social problems that occur simultaneously (e.g., health, air pollution, urban heat island, institutional fragility, social inequality and poverty) is hardly quantifiable and predictable. Moreover, current approaches in natural and social sciences are only starting to be prepared for the study of this type of wide ranging, simultaneous and systemic problems.

Governments and society are much less prepared for facing such problems, in part due to knowledge gaps and lack of a more comprehensive representation of risk. Dealing with several white and a few black swans at the same time may topple otherwise sufficient and adequate governmental and social capacities. Adequate impact and risk assessment are necessary for informing decision-making about critical issues and for developing effective risk management and risk reduction strategies (Dillon et al., 2009; Grossi & Kunreuther, 2005; Pollard et al., 2008). This is particularly challenging when it involves the analysis and modelling of complex systems and their interactions, which are characterized by fragmented information, incomplete knowledge and sometimes by what has been described as "unknown unknowns" (Oreskes et al., 1994; Spiegelhalter & Riesch, 2011; Walker et al., 2013). Such is the case of some of the most pressing socioenvironmental problems humanity is currently facing and will continue to do so for at least this century.

Catastrophic events are likely to be more frequent in a world in which socioenvironmental systems are pushed to their limits. Economic development and high levels of socioeconomic connectivity can quickly transform local shocks into global issues (Barnosky et al., 2011; Hansen et al., 2011; Lenton et al., 2019; Rockström et al., 2009). This has been illustrated by several financial and economic crises over the past decades, by terrorism which acts exclusively at local scales but that translates to global policies, also by environmental issues such as the impact of plastics on the global ocean, and of course, pollution and climate change.

One of the attributes defining Black Swans is that it is unpredictable because nothing in the past can convincingly point to its possibility (Taleb, 2007), or more broadly "nothing in our knowledge can convincingly point to its possibility" (Aven, 2013). Thus, the existence of a black swan depends on who is experiencing it and in their scientific and technical capacities which affect the ability to generate coordinated and coherent governmental and societal response. This also holds for the length and darkness of a shadow a single white swan or a flock of them could cast.

Given the high levels of socioeconomic connectivity such events will not be contained by political boundaries. As such, global risk reduction strategies should include closing the gaps in development, education and technology within and between countries. In the case of climate change and other global socioenvironmental problems, empirical or observational examples that may serve as analogues which could help guiding decision-making will be much more scarce or impossible. Moreover, the horizon needed to consider for policymaking is much longer than for a pandemic such as Covid-19 and the delay between the time actions are implemented and their results are seen may be quite long.

Information for supporting decision-making may also strongly depend on models with incomplete knowledge, substantial assumptions and high-levels of uncertainty. These characteristics can generate divergent perceptions about the problem and the correct way of dealing with it among different actors, as well as ambiguity about what is known or knowable. Such characteristics can introduce more complexity for decision-making, higher political costs and difficulties for generating coordinated and coherent responses and thus amplify risks and hamper effective action and optimal strategies. This has been repeatedly illustrated by the lack of success in international climate negotiations.

4.6 Conclusion

Addressing problems such as climate change and pandemics require global cooperation and coordination. Covid-19 provides us with an example of a predictable, but rare event for which we should be better prepared next time. In this chapter, I have argued that the lessons of the pandemic can be extended to the problem of climate change: catastrophic outcomes might result from predictable events and processes. It is the complex interaction between predictable events, the "White Swans", that can lead to otherwise unpredictable compound events, the "Black Swan". This pandemic should help us better assess how confident we should be about current estimates about the consequences of global socioenvironmental issues.

Luckily for mankind, globalization has not just made the spread of viruses easier, but also the means of communication. Information spreads just as well, so that news about virus outbreaks, preventive measures and therapies can be coordinated on the same global scale. After the onset of the Covid-19 pandemic, medical researchers worldwide as well as pharmaceutical companies join forces to come up with a vaccine. Whereas the traditional development of vaccines takes at least 10–15 years, the current prospects for a Corona vaccine are such that it might be available within 9 months from the emergence of the virus. That is a more than ten-fold increase in speed, spurred on by the seriousness of a worldwide catastrophe. This is a hopeful lesson for climate policy.

The world is currently much better equipped with technology, knowledge and science than in any previous time in history. This has made and will continue to make societies less vulnerable and more able to respond and adapt to environmental problems. However, we should also learn that problems that may be predictable and manageable in isolation, their interaction with other issues and natural and human systems may end up producing unpredictable, very costly and perhaps hardly manageable global issues.

References

Adler, M., Anthoff, D., Bosetti, V., et al. (2017). Priority for the worse-off and the social cost of carbon. *Nature Climate Change, 7*, 443–449.

Anthoff, D., & Tol, R. S. J. (2012). Schelling's conjecture on climate and development: A test. In *Climate change and common sense: Essays in honour of tom schelling* (pp. 260–274). Oxford University Press.

Anthoff, D., Estrada, F., & Tol, R. S. J. (2016). Shutting down the thermohaline circulation. *American Economic Review, 106*(5), 602–606.

Aven, T. (2013). On the meaning of a black swan in a risk context. *Safety Science, 57*, 44–51.

Barnosky, A. D., Matzke, N., Tomiya, S., et al. (2011). Has the Earth's sixth mass extinction already arrived? *Nature, 471*, 51–57.

Botzen, W. J. W., Estrada, F., & Tol, R. S. J. (2020). Methodological issues in natural disaster loss normalisation studies. *Environmental Hazards, 20*, 1–4.

Botzen, W. J. W., Duijndam, S., & van Beukering, P. (2021). Lessons for climate policy from behavioral biases towards COVID-19 and climate change risks. *World Development, 137*, 105214.

Brooks, D. R., & Boeger, W. A. (2019). Climate change and emerging infectious diseases: Evolutionary complexity in action. *Current Opinion in Systems Biology, 13*, 75–81.

Cheng, V. C. C., Lau, S. K. P., Woo, P. C. Y., & Kwok, Y. Y. (2007). Severe acute respiratory syndrome coronavirus as an agent of emerging and reemerging infection. *Clinical Microbiology Reviews, 20*(4), 660–694.

Cheng, W., Chiang, J. C. H., Zhang, D., et al. (2013). Atlantic meridional overturning circulation (AMOC) in CMIP5 models: RCP and historical simulations. *Journal of Climate, 26*(18), 7187–7197.

Colt, S. G., & Knapp, G. P. (2016). Economic effects of an ocean acidification catastrophe. *American Economic Review, 106*(5), 615–619.

Contini, C., Di Nuzzo, M., Barp, N., et al. (2020). The novel zoonotic COVID-19 pandemic: An expected global health concern. *The Journal of Infection in Developing Countries, 14*(03), 254–264.

Cox, P. M., Huntingford, C., & Williamson, M. S. (2018). Emergent constraint on equilibrium climate sensitivity from global temperature variability. *Nature, 553*, 319–322.

De Vos, J. (2020). The effect of COVID-19 and subsequent social distancing on travel behavior. *Transportation Research Interdisciplinary Perspectives, 5*, 100121.

Dillon, R. L., Liebe, R. M., & Bestafka, T. (2009). Risk-based decision making for terrorism applications. *Risk Analysis, 29*, 321–335.

Estrada, F., Tol, R. S. J., & Gay-García, C. (2015a). The persistence of shocks in GDP and the estimation of the potential economic costs of climate change. *Environmental Modelling & Software, 69*, 155–165.

Estrada, F., Wouter Botzen, W. J. W., & Tol, R. S. J. (2015b). Economic losses from US hurricanes consistent with an influence from climate change. *Nature Geoscience, 8*, 880–885.

Estrada, F., Botzen, W. J. W., & Tol, R. S. J. (2017a). A global economic assessment of city policies to reduce climate change impacts. *Nature Climate Change, 7*(6), 403–406.

Estrada, F., Tol, R. S. J., & Botzen, W. J. W. (2017b). Global economic impacts of climate variability and change during the 20th century. *PLoS One, 12*, e0172201.

Estrada, F., Tol, R. S. J., & Botzen, W. J. W. (2019). Extending integrated assessment models' damage functions to include adaptation and dynamic sensitivity. *Environ Model Softw, 121*, 104504.

Fan, V. Y., Jamison, D. T., & Summers, L. H. (2018). Pandemic risk: How large are the expected losses? *Bulletin of the World Health Organization, 96*(2), 129.

Field, C. B., Barros, V., Stocker, T. F., & Dahe, Q. (Eds.). (2012). *Managing the risks of extreme events and disasters to advance climate change adaptation: Special report of the intergovernmental panel on climate change.* Cambridge University Press.

Grinsted, A., Ditlevsen, P., & Christensen, J. H. (2019). Normalized US hurricane damage estimates using area of total destruction, 1900–2018. *Proceedings of the National Academy of Sciences, 116*(48), 23942–23946.

Grossi, P., & Kunreuther, H. (2005). *Catastrophe modeling: A new approach to managing risk* (Vol. 25). Springer Science & Business Media.

Haer, T., Botzen, W. W., Van Roomen, V., Connor, H., Zavala-Hidalgo, J., Eilander, D. M., & Ward, P. J. (2018). Coastal and river flood risk analyses for guiding economically optimal flood adaptation policies: A country-scale study for Mexico. *Philosophical Transactions of the Royal Society A: Mathematical, Physical and Engineering Sciences, 376*(2121), 20170329.

Hansen, J., Sato, M., Kharecha, P., & von Schuckmann, K. (2011). Earth's energy imbalance and implications. *Atmospheric Chemistry and Physics, 11*(24), 13421.

Hill, E. M., Tildesley, M. J., & House, T. (2017). Evidence for history-dependence of influenza pandemic emergence. *Scientific Reports, 7*, 43623.

Hoegh-Guldberg, O., Jacob, D., Bindi, M., Brown, S., Camilloni, I., Diedhiou, A., … Hijioka, Y. (2018). *Impacts of 1.5 C global warming on natural and human systems. Global warming of 1.5° C. An IPCC special report.* IPCC.

Ignjacevic, P., Botzen, W. W., Estrada, F., Kuik, O., Ward, P., & Tiggeloven, T. (2020). CLIMRISK-RIVER: Accounting for local river flood risk in estimating the economic cost of climate change. *Environmental Modelling & Software, 132*, 104784.

Lawrence, M. G., & Schäfer, S. (2019). Promises and perils of the Paris agreement. *Science, 364*(6443), 829–830.

Lenton, T. M., Rockström, J., Gaffney, O., Rahmstorf, S., Richardson, K., Steffen, W., & Schellnhuber, H. J. (2019). Climate tipping points—Too risky to bet against. *Nature, 575*, 592–595.

Mendelsohn, R. (2010). Climate change and economic growth. *Globalization and Growth, 60*, 24.

Mendelsohn, R., Prentice, I. C., Schmitz, O., Stocker, B., Buchkowski, R., & Dawson, B. (2016). The ecosystem impacts of severe warming. *American Economic Review, 106*(5), 612–614.

Millar, R. J., Fuglestvedt, J. S., Friedlingstein, P., Rogelj, J., Grubb, M. J., Matthews, H. D., … Allen, M. R. (2017). Emission budgets and pathways consistent with limiting warming to 1.5 C. *Nature Geoscience, 10*(10), 741–747.

Morens, D. M., & Fauci, A. S. (2020). Emerging pandemic diseases: How we got to COVID-19. *Cell, 182*, 1077–1092.

Nordhaus, W. D. (2010). The economics of hurricanes and implications of global warming. *Climate Change Economics, 1*(01), 1–20.

Nordhaus, W. D. (2011). The economics of tail events with an application to climate change. *Review of Environmental Economics and Policy, 5*(2), 240–257.

Nordhaus, W. (2018). Projections and uncertainties about climate change in an era of minimal climate policies. *American Economic Journal: Economic Policy, 10*(3), 333–360.

Oreskes, N., Shrader-Frechette, K., & Belitz, K. (1994). Verification, validation, and confirmation of numerical models in the earth sciences. *Science, 263*(5147), 641–646.

Poland, G. A., Jacobson, R. M., & Targonski, P. V. (2007). Avian and pandemic influenza: An overview. *Vaccine, 25*(16), 3057–3061.

Pollard, S. J., Davies, G. J., Coley, F., & Lemon, M. (2008). Better environmental decision making—Recent progress and future trends. *Science of the Total Environment, 400*(1–3), 20–31.

Ricke, K., Drouet, L., Caldeira, K., & Tavoni, M. (2018). Country-level social cost of carbon. *Nature Climate Change, 8*(10), 895–900.

Rockstrom, J., Steffen, W., Noone, K., Persson, A., Chapin, F. S., III, Lambin, E., T. M. Lenton, T. M., Scheffer, M., Folke, C., Schellnhuber, H., Nykvist, B., De Wit, C. A., Hughes, T., van der Leeuw, S., Rodhe, H., Sorlin, S., Snyder, P. K., Costanza, R., Svedin, U., Falkenmark, M., Karlberg, L., Corell, R. W., Fabry, V. J., Hansen, J., Walker, B., Liverman, D., Richardson, K., Crutzen, P., & Foley, J. (2009). Planetary boundaries:exploring the safe operating space for humanity. *Ecology and Society 14*(2), 32.

Rogelj, J., Popp, A., Calvin, K. V., Luderer, G., Emmerling, J., Gernaat, D., … Krey, V. (2018). Scenarios towards limiting global mean temperature increase below 1.5 C. *Nature Climate Change, 8*(4), 325.

Scarpino, S. V., & Petri, G. (2019). On the predictability of infectious disease outbreaks. *Nature Communications, 10*(1), 1–8.

Schellnhuber, H. J., Rahmstorf, S., & Winkelmann, R. (2016). Why the right climate target was agreed in Paris. *Nature Climate Change, 6*(7), 649–653.

Spiegelhalter, D. J., & Riesch, H. (2011). Don't know, can't know: Embracing deeper uncertainties when analysing risks. *Philosophical Transactions of the Royal Society A: Mathematical, Physical and Engineering Sciences, 369*(1956), 4730–4750.

Stern, N. (2013). The structure of economic modeling of the potential impacts of climate change: Grafting gross underestimation of risk onto already narrow science models. *Journal of Economic Literature, 51*(3), 838–859.

Stott, P. (2016). How climate change affects extreme weather events. *Science, 352*(6293), 1517–1518.

Taleb, N. N. (2007). *The black swan: The impact of the highly improbable* (Vol. 2). Random house.

Tol, R. S. (2009). The economic effects of climate change. *Journal of Economic Perspectives,* *23*(2), 29–51.

Tol, R. S. (2018). The economic impacts of climate change. *Review of Environmental Economics* *and Policy, 12*(1), 4–25.

Tol, R. S., Ebi, K. L., & Yohe, G. W. (2007). Infectious disease, development, and climate change: A scenario analysis. *Environment and Development Economics, 12*(5), 687–706.

Van den Bergh, J. C., & Botzen, W. J. (2014). A lower bound to the social cost of CO 2 emissions. *Nature Climate Change, 4*(4), 253–258.

Van den Bergh, J. C., & Botzen, W. J. W. (2015). Monetary valuation of the social cost of CO2 emissions: A critical survey. *Ecological Economics, 114*, 33–46.

Walker, W. E., Lempert, R. J., & Kwakkel, J. H. (2013). Deep uncertainty. In *Encyclopedia of* *operations research and management science* (pp. 395–402). Springer US.

Watts, N., Amann, M., Arnell, N., Ayeb-Karlsson, S., Beagley, J., Belesova, K., ... Capstick, S. (2020). The 2020 report of the lancet countdown on health and climate change: Responding to converging crises. *The Lancet, 397*, 129–170.

Weitzman, M. L. (2009). On modeling and interpreting the economics of catastrophic climate change. *The Review of Economics and Statistics, 91*(1), 1–19.

Zhenmin, L., & Espinosa, P. (2019). Tackling climate change to accelerate sustainable development. *Nature Climate Change, 9*(7), 494–496.

Francisco Estrada is a researcher in the Climate and Society research group at the Center for Atmospheric Sciences of the Universidad Nacional Autónoma de México (UNAM) and the Coordinator of the Climate Change Research Program of UNAM. He is also a visiting researcher at the Department of Environmental Economics, Institute for Environmental Studies (IVM), Vrije Universiteit Amsterdam. He was a contributing author for the Working Group II of the IPCC's Fourth Assessment Report and expert reviewer for the Working Group II contribution for the IPCC's Fifth Assessment Report. He has participated and coordinated research projects on the assessment of the potential impacts of climate change in agriculture, the economics of climate change and also on the generation of regional climate change scenarios.

Chapter 5
The Green Challenge for Central Banks and Households

Dirk Schoenmaker

Abstract Central banks should not be excluded from the list of responsible institutions to address climate change. They already have a bias in their balance sheets toward polluting industries, which should be reduced. Next, the government should design green policies that do not overburden middle class households.

5.1 Introduction

The focus on greening the economy is usually on governments, in their role as policymakers, and on firms and financial institutions, as powerful parties in the private sector. However, there is also an important role for central banks and households in meeting our society's green challenge. The ultimate goal of central banks is to safeguard the long-term prosperity of the economy, which is linked to a viable and green future. Similarly, households want to safeguard the living conditions of current and future generations. Accepting these goals allows the debate to move from the 'why' to the 'how' of making our economy more sustainable in the long-term.

For the transition to a low-carbon economy to occur, there are currently some strong biases at central banks and households. As carbon-intensive companies are also capital intensive, the ECB is overweight in corporate bonds issued by these companies and bank loans to these companies. On the household-side, the high-income and middle class households in the Western-European countries have carbon-intensive consumption patterns that are responsible for a disproportional large fraction of carbon emissions. This article shows how these biases can be addressed, while greening the economy. It also shows how climate policies can be designed in a neutral way for the middle class, both in terms of work and income.

D. Schoenmaker (✉)
Erasmus University, Bruegel & CEPR, Rotterdam, The Netherlands
e-mail: schoenmaker@rsm.nl

© The Author(s) 2022
A. Siegmann (ed.), *Climate of the Middle*, SpringerBriefs in Climate Studies,
https://doi.org/10.1007/978-3-030-85322-8_5

5.2   Who Should Act?

The Sustainable Development Goals (SDGs) form the world's business plan for a greener, more inclusive and sustainable future (UN, 2015). The SDG agenda is set by the United Nations, which suggests that the SDGs are the main responsibility of governments. However, there is growing recognition that all parties have a moral responsibility to contribute to achieving a sustainable future. We have a joint responsibility for the stewardship of our planet (Schoenmaker, 2020).

The stewardship for the environment is not without frictions or tensions. Until now, the focus has been on the large parties: on the governments at the policy side and companies and financial institutions on the private side. However, other parties should also act. Regarding policy, the European Central Bank (ECB) plays an important role in the economy. At the meta level, the ECB, like any central bank, aims for sustainable development of the economy. This means healthy development of the economy in the long run. Current levels of carbon emissions and biodiversity loss lead to unsustainable development of the economy (Loorbach et al., 2020).

The ECB can contribute in its monetary stability role as well as in its financial stability role to avert the economy from this unsustainable path. By taking a proactive role now (instead of relying on self-correcting markets), the ECB can avoid an 'I was wrong' admission of a future ECB president in, say, 2030. It appears that the ECB has currently a carbon bias in its monetary policy operations, which works against governments' ambitions to green the economy. The ECB should tilt, or more strongly target, its operations towards low-carbon corporate bonds and bank loans.

A tilt towards low-carbon bonds benefits financial stability. Bolton et al. (2020) identify climate change as the main risk for the stability of the financial system. This tail risk, which the authors call appropriately the 'Green Swan', is beyond the scope of this short article. Nevertheless, the ECB has an important role in the transition of the global financial system towards a financial system that works for people and planet (Loorbach et al., 2020).

In the private sector, the attention is also moving from the producers (companies) to the consumers (households). In the end, production and consumption equalise in the economy. So, both producers and consumers are responsible for the carbon footprint. But the carbon footprint is not distributed equally: high-income countries have a far larger footprint than middle- and low-income countries. A well-functioning price mechanism for carbon emissions, as proposed in Europe, can reduce carbon emissions. Also, to avoid relocation of carbon-intensive production activities, the European Commission is planning for a carbon border adjustment mechanism. The receipts of this carbon border tax could be channeled towards a climate fund to help low-income countries in their transition towards a low-carbon economy.

Within countries, the high-income group consumes up to half of the carbon budget. To ensure a just transition towards a low-carbon economy, a part of the receipts of the higher carbon taxes can be used to compensate the lower- and middle-income groups. Another part can be used for retraining. In this way, workers can transfer smoothly from 'brown' to 'green' sectors of the economy.

5.3   Greening Monetary Policy

The core task of the European Central Bank, as any central bank, is to support the economy. Its primary responsibility is defined as achieving price stability to keep the economy on a stable path. Without prejudice to price stability, the ECB should also support the general economic policies of the European Union (Article 127 of the Treaty on the Functioning of the European Union).

A focal point in the EU's general economic policies is the European Green Deal, which is endorsed by the European Council and the European Parliament (European Commission, 2019). Interestingly, the European Union has combined its COVID-recovery policies and green policies into a green recovery programme (European Council, 2020). As governments can only spend their money once (assuming there are limits to their borrowing), it makes sense to aim for a green recovery instead of general economic stimulus today and green stimulus in a few years time. Why finance a business-as-usual approach first and only later phase out the climate negative part of this business and stimulate the green part? You may as well start by stimulating the green part from the outset.

The same logic applies to the ECB. With its non-standard monetary policy operations, such as the Assets Purchases Programme under Quantitative Easing and the Targeted Long-Term Refinancing Operations (TLTROs), the ECB aims to stimulate the economy in order to get inflation close to its 2% target. The ECB has a long-standing policy of market neutrality. But there is evidence that the market has a bias towards carbon-intensive companies (Matikainen et al., 2017). As carbon-intensive companies, like oil and gas companies and car manufacturers, are typically capital intensive (Doda, 2016), market indexes for corporate bonds are overweighted in high-carbon companies. By taking assets proportional to the market index, the ECB is thus not climate neutral in the implementation of its monetary policy. Even worse, by doing so it is working *against* the European Green Deal. In a similar way, TLTROs refinance banks, which are still geared towards lending to SMEs and corporations that to a large extent operate in the carbon-intensive 'brown' economy.

The challenge is to let the ECB support the green recovery in a general way, without being dragged into specific green policies. The latter is the realm of elected politicians. In Schoenmaker (2021) I derive two main conditions for greening monetary policy. These conditions are a general approach (to avoid politically sensitive decisions on specific sectors and companies) and a broad asset and collateral base (to avoid distortions of monetary transmission). To satisfy both conditions, I propose a tilting approach for a central bank's direct asset holdings (related to official reserves or asset purchases under quantitative easing) and collateral holdings (related to monetary policy operations).[1] The basic idea of the tilting approach is to shift the composition of the ECB's asset and collateral portfolio towards low-carbon assets. The ECB can do that by increasing the proportion of low-carbon assets and

---

[1] Central banks grant loans to banks against collateral in their monetary policy operations.

at the same time reducing the proportion of high-carbon assets (see Schoenmaker, 2021, for details).

Another proposal is not just tilting, but targeting the ECB's TLTROs towards green lending. Green TLTROs are refinancing operations that provide banks with cheap funding if they lend in accordance with the EU's taxonomy of green activities (Van't Klooster & Van Tilburg, 2020). This approach is very powerful in steering funding towards the green sector of the economy.

The main barrier to green monetary policy is orthodox thinking – the ECB should only stimulate the economic recovery. The European Commission and Council have repeatedly stated their aim to combat climate change by reducing carbon emissions; the latest is the European green deal. This climate framework can be considered as the EU's general economic policies to protect the environment. European Parliament members have repeatedly asked questions to the (former) ECB president about the ECB's (lack of) carbon policies (see, for example, Draghi, 2018). It could be argued that the ECB's carbon policy in its monetary policy operations framework should be discussed (and perhaps also approved) by the European Parliament.

5.4 Greening Consumption

A widely used definition of sustainable development is in the Brundtland report (1987). The report defines sustainable development as *"development that meets the needs of the present without compromising the ability of future generations to meet their own needs"*. The Brundtland report reinforces the idea that sustainability is of concern to future generations. Households want to safeguard the living conditions of current and future generations by 'greening' their consumption.

In reducing the carbon-footpring of consumption, a separate challenge is to make this transition possible without increasing inequality. The idea of a 'just transition' stresses the need to ensure that efforts to steer society towards a lower carbon future are underpinned by attention to issues of equity and justice: to those currently without access to reliable energy supplies and living in energy poverty and to those whose livelihoods are affected by and depend on a fossil fuel economy (Newell & Mulvaney, 2013). Three elements of a just transition warrant attention:

1. Workers in high-carbon sectors;
2. Affordability for low- and middle-income groups;
3. Transition in low-income countries.

Workers in High-Carbon Sectors
Transition is about transformational change of the system rather than incremental change (Loorbach, 2010). The low-carbon transition of systems starts with new technologies and business models. It implies phasing out existing technologies and business models that cannot adapt. If markets are efficient, the Schumpeterian creative destruction can work on its own, as the highest return in the new sectors will enable the reallocation of workers. In reality, governments must help the workers to

retrain. The European Commission (2020) has mobilised € 145 billion for such a 'Just Transition Mechanism'.

In the destabilisation and disruption stages, governments often have the kneejerk reaction to help the business that is in trouble and/or to protect the jobs involved. But it is better to focus on helping the people and changing the system, as in the Danish model, where the labour market has a high level of flexibility when hiring, social welfare system and active employment policies. Together, these three components constitute what is known as the 'Flexicurity Model', combining the market economy with the traditional Scandinavian welfare state (see, for example, Jespersen et al., 2008).

Whereas national governments are the most powerful players with full access to taxation and regulation, subnational governments also have a role to play as transition often occurs at the regional level. Moreover, as the latter are closer to the citizens, they can play a key role in the acceptance of a transition. Effective interplay between the national and regional levels is crucial. A historical example is the transition from coal to gas in the Netherlands, which was funded by the revenues from gas exploration (Correljé & Verbong, 2004). When the coal mines in the south of the Netherlands were closed in the 1960s, the national government provided state aid to DSM (Dutch State Mines) to reform itself and offer alternative employment. The closure of the coal mines was prepared and executed jointly by the national government and the provincial government of Limburg. DSM is now one of the leading Dutch sustainable companies.

Affordability for Low- and Middle-Classes

An important mechanism to reduce carbon emissions is carbon pricing (Stern, 2008). Early adopters of carbon taxes are the Scandinavian countries in the 1990s, which have currently carbon taxes ranging from $50 to 130 per tCO_2 (ton of carbon dioxide). The Scandinavian experience shows that carbon pricing can be effective in changing behaviour and reducing carbon emissions. Åkerfeldt and Hammar (2015), for example, report that the gradual increase from €27 per tCO_2 in 1991 to €123 per tCO_2 in 2013 led to a shift in the energy mix from fossil fuels towards biofuels as well as heating of apartments by district heating (fuelled by household waste and various wood residues) in Sweden. The result was a reduction in carbon emissions of 23 per cent, without a negative impact on economic growth.

However, carbon taxes also increase the energy bill of households, which is not evenly distributed. Oxfam (2020) calculates that the high-income group is responsible for a substantial part of carbon emissions. Table 5.1 illustrates that nearly half of the total carbon emissions is due to the richest 10% in 2015. This high figure is stable from 1990 to 2015.

So, the high-income group contributes significantly to emissions. Part of the collected carbon taxes can be used to compensate the lower- and middle-income groups. Households can then afford low-carbon solutions for their consumption goods, housing and mobility and make their own choices as well. The change in income tax can be fine-tuned to arrange a more or less income-neutral transition for the lower-and middle-income groups. The high-income groups, which is

Table 5.1 Share of total carbon emissions (2015 figures)

Global income groups	Share of total carbon emissions
Top 10%	49%
Middle 40%	44%
Bottom 50%	7%
Total	100%

Source: Oxfam (2020)

responsible for nearly half of the emissions, would then bear the brunt of the carbon taxes. Importantly, the compensation should not be used for subsidies to buy fossil-fuel products.

Using energy-linked subsidies or taxes for households is not new. The IMF reports that pre-tax energy subsidies for fossil fuels amount to $333 billion, which is 0.4 per cent of world GDP in 2015 (Coady et al., 2017). They are usually aimed at keeping fuel affordable for low-income households, but as subsidies on carbon-based fuels they are counterproductive and a highly inefficient way to provide support to low-income households.

Another bias is the near exemption of the large industry in some countries to protect their international competitive position. In the Netherlands, for example, households (and SMEs) are paying energy taxes which are more or less in line with the environmental damage in the form of carbon emissions and air pollution. However, the big industrial users of energy pay only about 10% per cent of the appropriate energy tax (Bollen et al., 2019). This should be increased towards the full rate. A European carbon border tax can prevent relocation of activities (see below).

Transition in Low-Income Countries
The carbon footprint is not distributed equally between countries: high-income countries have a far larger footprint than middle- and low-income countries. An increasing carbon price, as proposed in Europe, can reduce carbon emissions in Europe. To avoid relocation of production activities, the European Commission (2019) is planning for a carbon border adjustment mechanism. This carbon border tax would then be based on the carbon-intensity of the imported product or service.

As the developed countries have already used a large part of the global carbon budget since the Industrial Revolution, it is fair that these countries help the developing countries to transfer rapidly to a low-carbon economy (and thus avoid a high-carbon economic development). This is in the joint interest of developed and developing countries, as global warming due to carbon emissions is a global threat.

The Paris Agreement does not only contain provisions for reducing carbon emissions, but also provisions for financial resources to assist developing countries in implementing these reductions. Notwithstanding these pledges, the developed countries have, to date, not kept their promise to fill the Climate Change Fund. An alternative might be that the European Union uses its receipts from the carbon border adjustment to fund the Climate Change Fund. This will speed up the low-carbon transition in low-and middle-income countries in two ways: a substantial carbon border tax for carbon-intensive products (exported to the European Union) and a subsidy for adopting low-carbon technologies.

Acemoglu et al. (2012) show that optimal policies to redirect technical change to cleaner technology are a mix of carbon taxes (to make dirty technology more expensive) and subsidies for clean technology (to redirect technological research and development). Developing breakthrough technologies should be one of the main priorities for the EU, if it wants to be instrumental in reducing worldwide CO_2-emissions.

5.5 Conclusion

While the low-carbon transition tends to focus on governments and private parties as key players, this article shows that central banks and households also have a role to play. The starting point is that carbon emissions are not equally distributed. The ECB appears to have a carbon bias in its asset and collateral portfolio. Next to that, the high-income group is a major contributor to the consumption-based carbon footprint.

The solutions described in this chapter reduce carbon emissions and mitigate potential inequalities. Climate policies can be designed in a neutral way for the low- and middle-income groups, both in terms of work and income. In such a 'just transition' scenario, the social and environmental goals of sustainable development can be jointly achieved. An appropriate narrative of such a just transition is crucial in the political discourse.

This narrative can be on the following lines: We need to reduce carbon emissions to address global warming which has major consequences for us and our children. Carbon pricing is a tool to transition from a high to a low-carbon economy. As governments do not need extra money, the receipts from carbon pricing can be used to guide the transition of workers from high to low carbon sectors and to compensate low- and middle-income groups for higher consumption prices.

References

Acemoglu, D., Aghion, P., Bursztyn, L., & Hemous, D. (2012). The environment and directed technical change. *American Economic Review, 102*(1), 131–166.

Åkerfeldt, S., & Hammar, H. (2015). *CO2 Taxation in Sweden: Experiences of the past and future challenges*. Revue Projet Journal 2015–09.

Bollen, J., Brink, C., Romijn, G., Tijm, J., & Vollebergh, H. (2019). *Verantwoording behorend bij de Policy Brief: Economische effecten van CO2-beprijzing – Varianten vergeleken* (Accountability for the Policy Brief: Economic effects of CO2-prices – scenarios compared). Central Planning Agency and Planning Agency for the Environment.

Bolton, P., Després, M., da Silva, L. A. P., Samama, F., & Svartzman, R. (2020). *The green swan: Central banking and financial stability in the age of climate change*. Bank for International Settlements.

Brundtland Report. (1987). *Our Common Future*. The United Nations World Commission on Environment and Development, United Nations.

Coady, D., Parry, I., Sears, L., & Shang, B. (2017). How large are global fossil fuel subsidies? *World Development, 91*, 11–27.

Correljé, A., & Verbong, G. (2004). The transition from coal to gas: Radical change of the Dutch gas system. In B. Elzen, F. Geels, & K. Greens (Eds.), *System innovation and the transition to sustainability* (pp. 114–134). Edward Elgar.

Doda, B. (2016). *Sector-level carbon intensity distribution*. Centre for Climate Change Economics and Policy Working Paper No. 281.

Draghi, M. (2018). *Letter to the European Parliament*. L/MD/18/207, Frankfurt, 12 June.

European Commission. (2019). *The European green deal*. Communication from the Commission to the European Parliament and the European Council, COM(2019) 640 final, Brussels.

European Commission. (2020). *A key tool to ensure that the transition towards a climate-neutral economy happens in a fair way, leaving no one behind*, Press Release, 14 January.

European Council. (2020). *EU leaders agree on EU recovery plan and budget 2021–2027*, European Council Conclusions, 21 July.

Jespersen, S., Munch, J., & Skipper, L. (2008). Costs and benefits of Danish active labour market programmes. *Labour Economics, 15*(5), 859–884.

Loorbach, D. (2010). Transition management for sustainable development: A prescriptive, complexity-based governance framework. *Governance: An International Journal of Policy, Administration, and Institutions, 23*(1), 161–183.

Loorbach, D., Schoenmaker, D., & Schramade, W. (2020). *Finance in transition: Guiding principles for a positive finance transition* (RSM series on positive change volume 3). Rotterdam School of Management, Erasmus University Rotterdam.

Matikainen, S., Campiglio, E., & Zenghelis, D. (2017). *The climate impact of quantitative easing*. Grantham Research Institute on Climate Change and the Environment, Policy Paper.

Newell, P., & Mulvaney, D. (2013). The political economy of the just transition. *Geographical Journal, 179*(2), 132–140.

Oxfam. (2020). *The carbon inequality era*. Oxfam and Stockholm Environment Institute, Joint Research Report.

Schoenmaker, D. (2020). *The impact economy: Balancing profit and impact*, Working Paper 04, Bruegel.

Schoenmaker, D. (2021). Greening monetary policy. *Climate Policy, 21*(4), 581–592.

Stern, N. (2008). The economics of climate change. *American Economic Review: Papers and Proceedings, 98*(2), 1–37.

United Nations. (2015). *UN sustainable development goals – Transforming our World: The 2030 Agenda for sustainable development*, A/RES/70/1, New York.

Van't Klooster, J., & Van Tilburg, R. (2020). *Targeting a sustainable recovery with green TLTRO*. Positive Money Europe, Brussels and Sustainable Finance Lab.

Dirk Schoenmaker is Professor of Banking and Finance at Rotterdam School of Management, Erasmus University Rotterdam, a Non-Resident Fellow at Bruegel and Research Fellow at the Centre for European Policy Research (CEPR). He has published in the areas of sustainable finance, central banking, financial supervision and stability and European financial integration. Dirk is author of 'Governance of International Banking: The Financial Trilemma' (Oxford University Press) and co-author of the textbooks 'Principles of Sustainable Finance' (Oxford University Press) and 'Financial Markets and Institutions: A European Perspective' (Cambridge University Press). He earned his PhD in economics at the London School of Economics. Dirk was Dean of the Duisenberg school of finance from 2009 to 2015. He is a regular consultant for the IMF, the OECD and the European Commission.

Chapter 6
Corporate Taxation in a Circular Economy

Jan Gooijer

Abstract A circular economy leads to challenges for the system of corporate taxation. However, there exist already a legal rationale for the levy of corporate tax in a circular economy. Such a rationale, a convincing *raison d'être* for corporate taxation in a circular economy, contributes to the legitimacy for a green corporate tax. I explore some new measures in corporate taxation that are consistent with a circular economy.

6.1 Introduction

With the European Green Deal the European Committee has set the agenda towards a sustainable economy. The fight against climate change, environmental pollution, the loss of biodiversity and the exhaustive use of resources requires a radical change in the current economic model. According to the Committee, that current model should be replaced by a model based on the concept of circularity. The profit-oriented free-market economy will have to change into a circular economy "that is restorative and regenerative by design, and which aims to keep products, components and materials at their highest utility and value at all times, distinguishing between technical and biological cycles", see MacArthur Foundation (2015). It is clear that a successful transformation to a circular economy requires fundamental changes in the functioning of markets and the way in which market participants interact. As Backes (2017) rightly pointed out, the Committee's agenda requires 'a systemic change'. The relationship between market, state and society should be reconsidered and the boundaries of market forces will have to be redefined.

In order to achieve such new equilibrium between state and market, it is necessary to reconsider the fundamentals of various areas of law. Gerbrandy (2017), for example, stated that the basic principles and objectives of competition law are incompatible with the requirements of a circular economy. When it comes to tax

J. Gooijer (✉)
Faculty of Law, Vrije Universiteit Amsterdam, Amsterdam, The Netherlands
e-mail: j.gooijer@vu.nl

© The Author(s) 2022
A. Siegmann (ed.), *Climate of the Middle*, SpringerBriefs in Climate Studies,
https://doi.org/10.1007/978-3-030-85322-8_6

law, the emphasis has so far been on the introduction of energy and environmental taxes. In the area of direct taxation a fundamental discussion about the principles of the tax system and the structure of that system in the light of environmental issues is yet to be initiated, see Traversa (2020). Corporation tax 'touches on the distribution of functions and weights between the State and the economy' and the systemic change into a circular economy requires us to evaluate whether the corporate tax system contributes to the desired balance, see Vogel (1988).

6.2 Dilemmas of Corporate Taxation in a Circular Economy

Two examples from the world of corporate taxation will make clear what the potential challenges are for the functioning of firms and their tax bill in a circular economy. The first example is that of real estate. If real estate development becomes more sustainable, the economic lifetime of buildings and the residual value will increase significantly. Buildings have to become more durable if we want to limit the resource use in the built environment that has now a standard lifetime of, say, 50 years. And after demolition, the re-use of existing materials increases the residual value of the real estate. In this situation of sustainable real estate development, cradle-to-cradle, depreciation is greatly affected: the normal tax deductible depreciation will be smaller or nil. At the same time, the cost for an office building or industrial site might not have changed much, or might even increase.

The second example is that of the ownership structures of assets and the financing structure of business operations. Under a conventional business model, an acquired product may be presented as an asset on the balance sheet, providing collateral for lenders. Under a circular business model, the buyer may not own the product in the conventional sense, resulting in less collateral for the lenders and, thus, higher interest costs. Furthermore, such a reduced asset base results in a reduced tax deductible depreciation. Depreciation on the products owned by the service provider will be included in the service payments, reducing EBITDA[1] of the buyer. Higher interest costs and reduced EBITDA will both have a negative impact on the tax deductible amount under EBITDA-interest deduction rules.

In both examples, tax deductible items are reduced, which leads to a higher effective tax rate. Regardless of one's views on the appropriate level of corporate taxation, this does raise issues for the legislator, as it leads to changes in the tax base, differences between countries and new areas for tax arbitrage. Thus, we need to raise the question of how corporate taxation in a circular economy should be structured.

---

[1] EBITDA is a commonly used measure of profitability: Earnings Before Interest, Taxes, Depreciation and Amortization.

6.3 A Legitimate Green Corporate Tax

The principles that underlie the tax system and which, in an optimal situation, would lead to a system that, taking into account the current social and economic circumstances, is perceived as fair and legitimate, must be reassessed regularly, see Avi-Yonah (2004). What principles should a green corporate tax be based on?

The underlying rationale for the corporate taxes that are currently in place is difficult to establish. There are several legal grounds, the hierarchy of which changes according to the perspective presented, see Bird (2002) and Boer and Elsweier (2019). If the relationship between corporate tax and income tax at the level of the shareholder is taken into account, the justification for levying corporate tax is what is called the support function in connection with the income tax, which is based on the 'ability to pay'-principle. Without a corporate tax, levying income tax on business profits and income from capital becomes largely illusory. From that perspective, corporate tax is 'backstopping the personal tax' (Bird, 2002).

However, if the independence of the company is emphasized, and there is much to be said for this given the independent operation of large multinationals, then the corporate tax cannot be justified by relying on the maintenance of a properly functioning income tax (Brooks, 2003). The question then is what can be regarded as the guiding principles of corporate tax. Four arguments for the existence of a corporate tax can be derived from legal scholarship, to which I add a fifth one, the principle that also underpins environmental taxes.

The arguments are (i) the principle of privileged acquisition, (ii) the benefits principle, (iii) the prosperity principle, and (iv) the principle of balance of power. I add to these four principles a fifth one, (v) the polluter pays or damage principle. This is the principle that underpins environmental taxes, but in my view may also play a valuable role as a legal rationale for a 'renewed' corporate tax. I will briefly elaborate on these five principles below.

The Principle of Privileged Acquisition

According to the principle of privileged acquisition, the amount of tax due on income or capital, should be in proportion to the effort that is made to acquire that income or capital. A tax on income received without any significant activity being carried out is neutral in the sense that the tax will not cause the taxpayer to change his or her behavior, activities or investments.

Corporate tax is a tax on what is called pure economic profits ('rent' or 'excess profits'). Pure economic profits are the earnings in excess of the earnings needed to cover all the firm's costs (the costs on labor and on capital, including the opportunity costs on equity), see *inter alia* Brooks (2003) and De Langen (1954). Such profits would not have been achieved in a fully transparent and well-functioning free market but arise 'whenever a firm has a degree of monopoly power in a market, is exploiting naturel resources, is operating in a regulated industry, or has some unique location or other business advantage' (Brooks, 2003). Therefore, taxing such profits is justified under the principle of privileged acquisition.

The Benefits Principle

A company benefits from public expenditure. It makes advantage of the legal system from which it derives its legal personality and which makes it possible for the company to participate on the marketplace. Furthermore, companies benefit from a countries educational and healthcare system, infrastructure etc. Based on that fact, it is justified to levy corporate tax, see Gooijer (2019).

The Prosperity Principle

The third principle that is considered important in the design of corporate taxation is what it referred to as the prosperity principle (Brüll, 1964). The argument is that corporate taxation should be limited because it has a negative effect on the level of investments and future growth of companies, which has a negative effect on economic development, employment opportunities and, in general, on prosperity.

Obviously, this principle limits the scope of the principle of privileged acquisition: despite the fact that there is windfall profit (rent) and in theory a levy of 100% of these windfall profits is justified, the levy must be limited for the benefit of further economic development and investments in, for example, research and development. Therefore the prosperity principle mitigates the principle of privileged acquisition and ensures that 'sufficient' profit remains for (re)investment and economic growth.

The Principle of Balance of Power

A fourth rationale, particularly relied on to justify corporate taxation in the United States, is based on the economic power of corporate management, see Avi-Yonah (2004). I want to refer to the principle as the balance of power principle. Avi-Yonah argued that this rationale is of importance to today's corporation taxes. In the context of the question of the role of corporate tax in the transformation to a circular economy for which a changed relationship between state and market seems necessary, it is interesting to discuss Avi-Yonah's arguments in a bit more detail. The line of reasoning is as follows.

Because of their position and the financial resources companies often have at their disposal, corporate managers have power in the sense that they have the ability to influence the behavior of others. Avi-Yonah pointed to sociological literature from which it follows that this influence extends into three areas. First, political power, because corporate management can influence political decision-making. There is also economic power, which manifests itself mainly in relation to the employees and the communities in which companies are established (for example, the establishment of a factory and the location of the head office). Thirdly, especially if there is a monopoly or oligopoly, the corporate manager has power over customers. The dominance the American tech giants have, is a perfect example of this.

What is the problem of the (possible) dominant power of corporate managers? According to Avi-Yonah, there are 'two principal arguments why a liberal democratic state should curb excessive accumulations of private power'. The first argument concerns democracy, the second the principle of equality. For a democracy to function optimally, it is necessary that there is no great accumulation of power among persons or organizations that do not have to render public account for the use of that power, Avi-Yonah argues. And private concentrations of power can affect equality within a society, equality in the sense that 'every social "sphere" should have its own appropriate distributive principles and that possession of goods relevant to one sphere should not automatically translate into dominance in other spheres as well.' Concentration of power in one sphere should not lead to disruption of relationships in other "spheres" of society, such as politics.

Corporate tax could play a role in countering excessive concentrations of power, resulting in the two aforementioned problems. After all, the levying of corporate tax reduces the financial possibilities of corporate managers, which has a direct effect on the position they occupy. Avi-Yonah: 'Whatever the economic incidence of the corporate tax, from this perspective its most immediate burden falls on corporate management, and not surprisingly, they are the strongest supporters of corporate tax repeal.'

The Damage Principle
The economic rationale for environmental taxes such as CO_2-taxes and waste taxes is that of repairing market failure, based on the theories of the economist Pigou, see Parry (2012) and Stancil (2010). For example, costs associated with CO_2-emissions in a properly functioning market would be included in the cost price. Involvement of the state is necessary for the proper functioning of the market.

The legal foundation of environmental taxes - and of environmental law in general - is found in the 'polluter pays' principle, see Bervoets (2019). That principle, which is also laid down in Article 191, paragraph 2 of the Treaty on the Functioning of the European Union, expresses the notion that it is reasonable for polluters to bear the costs of pollution control and elimination, because they caused that pollution.

In my opinion, both principles are suitable for underpinning corporate taxation in a circular economy. Restoring a market failure can be seen as the economic equivalent of the legal principle of privileged acquisition (which in fact deals with the effect of, for example, monopoly positions). The polluter pays principle justifies the levy of corporate tax on profits from activities that causes damage to the environment. Following Grapperhaus (1995), I will use below the expression 'damage principle', because it better expresses the premise that in general the conduct of a business should not lead to damage to public goods and that, insofar as damage does occur, that damage should be compensated.

Summing up
There is not one decisive legal rationale for corporate taxation. In my opinion, however, the above-mentioned principles together have sufficient persuasive strength for the existence of corporate tax systems, also in a circular economy. When looking for a - composite - legal rationale for corporate tax in a circular economy, these motives must therefore be considered in conjunction with one another.

It is particularly relevant that the operation of the principle of privileged acquisition is limited by the principle of prosperity and that the balance of power principle seems to supplement the principle of privileged acquisition. While the latter permits the levy of tax based on the mere fact that a beneficial position such as a monopoly has resulted in the pure economic profit, the former adds that corporate tax is justified to control the influence of corporate managers. Leaving pure economic profit unencumbered may lead to excessive concentrations of power with the possibility to exert undue influence in areas other than the economic realm.

On the basis of the damage principle, in particular those profits should be taxed that arise from activities that (potentially) cause damage to the environment. Under the damage principle, profits from activities that do not harm people and planet could be taxed less heavily. Furthermore, given the relationship between personal income tax and corporate tax and in accordance with the support function of the corporate tax, any measure introduced in corporate tax system should likewise apply to personal income taxes, as far as business profits are concerned.

6.4   Corporate Tax Design in a Circular Economy

It is clear that the principles discussed above must be translated into concrete measures in which conflicting principles must be weighed up. Furthermore, the effectiveness and feasibility of these possible measures should be considered. Below I outline some measures that I think are worth investigating further. First, I deal with the question how to differentiate between circular and conventional business activities. Then I will introduce a possible measure for the benefit of circular business operations that I believe deserves further research.

Differentiating Between Businesses

A green corporate tax differentiates between sustainable business operations and operations that cannot be qualified as such. To differentiate between these forms of business operations the approach in the 'Regulation on the establishment of a framework to facilitate sustainable investment' may be helpful.[2] That regulation 'establishes the criteria for determining whether an economic activity qualifies as environmentally sustainable for the purposes of establishing the degree to which an investment is environmentally sustainable'. The regulation recognizes six environmental objectives that are taken into account to establish whether a given economic activity is to be regarded environmental sustainable: mitigation and adaptation of climate change; sustainable use of water; transition to a circular economy; prevention of pollution; and the protection and restoration of biodiversity. An economic activity is considered environmentally sustainable if it (a) makes a substantial contribution to one of these environmental objectives, (b) does not seriously affect it, (c) meets technical screening criteria set by the European Commission and (d) complies with international guidelines on business and human rights. The technical screening criteria are included in the Technical Annex of the report of the EU

---

[2] This is laid down in Regulation (EU) 2020/852 of the European Parliament and of the Council of 18 June 2020, on the establishment of a framework to facilitate sustainable investment.

Technical Expert Group on Sustainable Finance (2019). The annex consists of 600 pages with detailed descriptions of business activities that are qualified as environmentally sustainable. This has been done as much as possible in line with existing EU regulations.

The framework provided by the regulation serves to promote sustainable investments. Public-interest entities[3] with at least 500 employees in 2021 will have to include information in their annual report from 2022 on the extent to which their activities can be considered environmentally sustainable within the meaning of the regulation. The statement should include the proportion of capital and operational expenditure related to those environmentally sustainable activities.[4]

This regulation forms an excellent starting point for 'green' measures in corporate taxation. The organizations to which the regulation applies already have the relevant data. For smaller organizations, it should be examined how activities can be efficiently classified in accordance with the guidelines laid down in the regulation.

A Capital and Labor Costs Allowance
A lower effective tax on green profits could obviously be achieved through a differentiation in the corporate tax rate. However, this may provide an approach that is too general, making an accurate and practically very complicated profit split necessary for companies with mixed activities. The focus could therefore be on the two factors that enable entrepreneurship and that can be specifically attributed to the relevant green activities: labor and capital. The effective rate on green profits is reduced by means of an (extra) deduction on capital, to the extent the capital is used for qualifying sustainable business activities and an extra deduction related to the labor costs that are related to these activities. The capital allowance stimulates the use of and investment in assets for sustainable activities, as well as investments in research and development. Employment in the sector is stimulated through the labor costs allowance. By allowing the deduction to consist of these two components, it is achieved that both labor and capital intensive sustainable companies can make use of the facility. In this way, it contributes to one of the goals of the European Commission's (2018) action plan.

Such a measure would in my view fit perfectly with a corporation tax redesigned to meet requirements of a circular economy, in alignment with the legal rationales of a corporation tax: the principles of privileged acquisition and balance of power, and the damage and well-being principle. I recall the two examples from above. Investments in real estate that is developed in accordance with the cradle-to-cradle principle benefit from the capital allowance, would lead to reduced tax deductible depreciation under current corporate tax systems. A capital allowance for such investments should at least eliminate that disadvantage. The same applies to the possible effect of product as a service models on tax deductibility of interest. An extra

---

[3] Entities as mentioned in Article 2, paragraph 1 of the Regulation 2013/34/EU of the European Parliament and of the Council on the annual financial statements, consolidated financial statements and related reports of certain types of undertakings.

[4] Article 8 Regulation (EU) 2020/852.

tax deductible amount on the capital used to finance sustainable business activities could erase possible negative consequences of changes in balance sheets and cash flow.

6.5 Conclusion

The challenges posed by the climate and environmental crisis require a critical evaluation of the entire legal system, including that of tax law. In my opinion, the basic principles of corporate taxation, supplemented by the damage principle, justify the introduction of special measures aimed at environmentally sustainable businesses. Therefore, further research into the possibility and effectiveness of a capital and labor cost allowance is recommended. By means of such an allowance, the negative effects of a changed balance sheet and cash flow position of sustainable business operations could be counteracted or even turned into a benefit, depending on the amount of the deduction. Such a capital and labor cost allowance would preferably be introduced throughout the European Union via a European directive in order to prevent tax competition between the member states.[5] The alternative may be to introduce a European corporate tax based on the above mechanism, though this may still be a long way off.

References

Avi-Yonah, R. S. (2004). Corporations, society, and the state: A defense of the corporate tax. *Virginia Law Review, 90*, 1195.
Backes, C. (2017). *Law for a circular economy, inaugural lecture* (p. 14). Eleven International Publishing.
Bervoets, P., et al. (2019). *Hoofdzaken milieuheffingen* (pp. 7–8). Kluwer.
Bird, R. M. (2002). Why tax corporations. *Bulletin for International Taxation, 56*(6), 201.
Boer, J. P., & Elsweier, F. J. (2019). Hinken op twee gedachten: over de rechtsgrond(en) van de Wet VPB 1969. In A. J. A. Stevens & J. L. van der Streek (Eds.), *De toekomst van de vennootschapsbelasting. Lessen uit 50 jaar Wet VPB 1969* (p. 31). Wolters Kluwer.
Brooks, K. (2003). Learning to live with an imperfect tax: A defense of the corporate tax. *U.B.C. Law Review, 36*, 636.
Brüll, D. (1964). *Objectieve en subjectieve aspecten van het fiscale winstbegrip* (p. 280). N.V. Uitgeverij FED.
de Langen, W. J. (1954). *De grondbeginselen van het Nederlandse belastingrecht, deel I*. Uitgever Samson, blz. 155.
Ellen Mac Arthur Foundation. (2015, December 9). *Towards a circular economy. Business rationale for an accelerated transition*. Ellen Mac Arthur Foundation

[5] Following the judgment of the ECJ of 23 April 2009, C-460/07, ECLI:EU:C:2009:254 *(Puffer)*, the benefit from a capital and wage bill allowance introduced by means of a directive, does not qualify as State aid as referred to in Article 107, paragraph 1 of the Treaty on the Functioning of the European Union.

European Commission. (2018). *Action plan: Financing sustainable growth, communication from the commission*, 8 March 2018, COM(2018) 97 final.

Gerbrandy, A. (2017). Circulaire economie en de grondslagen van het mededingsrecht. In C. Backes, J. Tieman, & N. Teesing (Eds.), *Met recht naar een circulaire economie* (p. 198). Boom Juridisch.

Gooijer, J. (2019). *Tax treaty residence of entities*. Kluwer Law International.

Grapperhaus, F. H. M. (1995). *Belasting op produktiefactoren* (p. 1525 e.v.). WFR.

Parry, I. W. H. et al. (2012). *Environmental tax reform: Principles from theory and practice to date*, IMF working paper, p. 7 et sec.;

Stancil, J. L. (2010). Taxes and sustainability. In J. A. F. Stoner & C. Wankel (Eds.), *Global sustainability as a business imperative. The Palgrave series on global sustainability* (p. 148 et sec). Palgrave.

Technical Expert Group on Sustainable Finance. (2019). *Taxonomy: Final report*, 9 March 2020.

Traversa, E. (2020). *The tax implications of global warming: Preparing for a change of climate* (p. 468). Intertax.

Vogel, K. (1988). The justification for taxation: A forgotten question. *The American Journal of Jurisprudence, 33*(19), 56.

Jan Gooijer is Assistant Professor Tax Law at the Vrije Universiteit Amsterdam and deputy-judge at the Rechtbank Noord-Holland. Jan obtained a PhD from the Vrije Universiteit Amsterdam for his thesis on the place of residence of companies under treaties for the avoidance of double taxation. Jan is board member of the Amsterdam Zuidas Institute for Financial Law and Company Law and participates in the research institute Climate Change, Corporations and the Law. He regularly contributes in various journals to discussions on national and international tax law. His current research focuses on the impact of the transition to circular business models for the tax obligations of enterprises. From 1997 to 2012 Jan worked as a tax advisor at PwC, with a specialisation in Dutch corporate income tax and international tax law.

Chapter 7
Climate Change in the Attention Arena of the Middle Class

Hans von Storch

Abstract Good intentions by the middle class are not always well guided and do not always lead to measurable or significant results. For example, efforts to limit greenhouse gas emissions may hold broad appeal but can still have negligible impact. Therefore, it is suggested to embark on "Apollo projects", which bundle the potential and willingness of the middle class. These projects should focus on the development of specific technologies, with economic advantages to support their spread throughout the world. Doing so will harness the middle class in support of greenhouse gas emission reductions in the gigaton-range. Such pan-national projects, for example, could address emission-free ship- or air-propulsion, the electrification of heating or of processes in the chemical industry.

7.1 Introduction

The middle class needs concerns, real or perceived, as part of life. In the absence of direct threats, such as war, hunger or viruses, then environmental deterioration is a well-received issue by the middle class, and allows for the development and practice of their good intentions.

In the following, first an understanding is introduced: what the "middle class" constitutes. This understanding is clearly a simplification; the middle class is an enormously complex social group, but I hope that some key features are covered well. In particular, I hope that it is clear on the dimension of accepting challenges of somehow "improving the world". Then, I look at the interruption brought by COVID-19 and at the challenge of the more indirect threat and cultural construct of the climate crisis.

The very real problem of anthropogenic climate change, and its anticipated solution as documented in the Paris agreement, is associated with an enormous quantitative challenge: namely the ending of all emissions of greenhouse gases by 2050, everywhere in the world, and for every purpose. Unfortunately, this is hardly

H. von Storch (✉)
Hamburg, Germany

understood by the middle class. When this quantitative challenge is not understood, the climate crisis cannot be handled. At the end of this article, it is suggested that we build on the goodwill of the middle class to focus our resources on *Apollo projects*. Such projects are needed to bring about technological advancements that could reduce greenhouse gas emissions in the gigaton-range.

7.2   The Middle Class and Its Worries

The term "middle class" goes with a variety of meanings. I will refer to that social stratum where people have a sufficient and secure income, but are not rich. Or, as Wikipedia summaries: *"the middle class as having a reasonable amount of discretionary income, so that they do not live from hand-to-mouth as the poor do. ... beginning at the point where people have roughly a third of their income left for discretionary spending after paying for basic food and shelter."* As such, a significant middle class emerged with the industrialization and with trade, mostly sometime in the nineteenth century.

Thus, I suggest, the members of the middle class do not suffer from significant, immediate and direct problems concerning income, housing and food. While most free resources of the middle class go into increasing income and security, part of their energy is used for developing a good and just lifestyle, and also to protect against dynamics which may threaten their income and security. These threats may be real, but they do not need to be so. In the nineteenth and twentieth centuries the threatening forces were perceived to be the 'underclass' portion of society and their requests for redistribution of wealth and privilege. These days, it could also be seen to be foreigners, perceived as questioning the middle classes' own identity, or superiority rooted in nationalism and racism.

In Europe – I will refer mostly to Northern Europe, which I have observed now for almost 70 years – this middle class became saturated sometime during the 1970s and 1980s. When conventional pressures, such as housing, labour, education and health, became less significant, a new reason of concern emerged, among them the request for a "natural" living milieu. The green motif established itself as a new bourgeois goal, see Radkau (2011).

Initially, attention was paid to the immediate environment (*milieu*), with a focus on air and water quality, the health of forests and local ecosystems, occupational health and safety, and natural reserves. But it also spread to concerns over radioactivity and nuclear power plants. Later, in the 1990s, the issue of climate change, with its various detrimental effects, became the overarching theme, covering not only the local challenges but also a global existential threat. Nowadays, in the beginning of the 2020s, most environmental concerns are attributed to anthropogenic climate change, although topics such as plastic in the sea or air quality are hardly climate issues.

This conceptualization of the middle class and its embracement of a green agenda represents a massive reduction in complexity. Substantial parts of the middle class are critical of the scientific explanation of anthropogenic climate change, but the majority is worried, see NOS (2020). I hope, however, that this reduction in complexity brings forward the significant dimension of the problem at hand, namely, how to effectively deal with the climate crisis.

The concern for climate change is large in the middle class but far from uniform, as an Austrian survey shows. According to this study, better financial status and higher education is associated with a tendency for a deeper concern for climate change ("*klimafreundliche Einstellung*"), whereas people with forced reduced working hours ("*Kurzarbeit*") rate climate change less significant, see Resch et al. (2020). This illustrates the duality of relative affluence and climate concerns quite well.

The issue of climate change thus has two dimensions. One is the change itself, whose reality is no longer questioned in science, with its mostly detrimental effects on the geophysical and ecological world. The other dimension constitutes the opportunity for people to build a better world, to use the free energy of the middle class constructively. In Germany, this dimension allows a post-Nazi generation to free itself from the perceived historical guilt of the past crimes against humanity, see Neiman (2019). For the members of the middle class it can be viewed as an active contribution to redeem the sins that the well-off people in the West have committed to the earth's climate.

Anthropogenic climate change is an abstract threat for almost all people. They would not know about it had they not been told about it by the media, by interest groups and scientists. Extreme events are summarily declared to represent this anthropogenic climate change, through every storm, heavy rainfall event and heat wave. At the same time, apocalyptic perspectives of climate change, of future desertification, migration, wars, sea level rise and associated coastal inundation, add to the perception of immediate catastrophe, even if much of these perspectives and interpretations are the result of exaggerations. Even so, they serve the purpose of creating concern and the providing the option of "saving the world".

7.3 Sentiment Can Reverse Quickly – The Virus

But then, suddenly, the virus came and brought back immediate and direct threats. People became ill, some died. It seems that in terms of the number of infected and diseased people, the present pandemic compares, at least for New York, to the pandemic of the Spanish flu of 1918–20, see Mandavilli (2020).

Not surprisingly, the issue of the virus gains very high attention in surveys about public concern. The levels of immediate concern for both the virus and the climate became comparable. A German newspaper, Der Spiegel, reported that a survey taken in the spring of 2020 in Germany showed younger people (*28–45 years old*) to rate climate change as the dominant challenge (50%), whereas a majority of 53% of those older than 45 years pointed to the pandemic, see Wahnbaeck (2020).

Indirect evidence of this abrupt change of attention away from climate to the pandemic, is illustrated in Fig. 7.1, which shows a substantial increase of the presence of "climate" in the monitored media from 2017 to 2019; with substantial

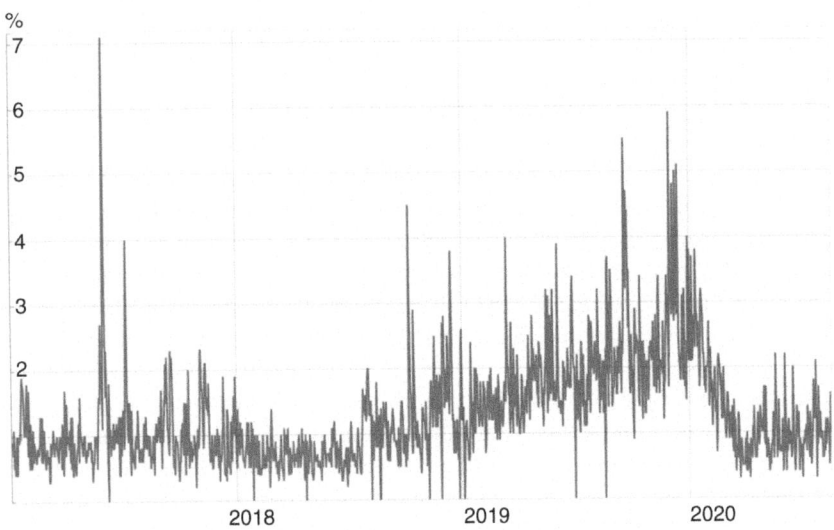

Fig. 7.1 Percentage of climate change related articles online in Europe. (Source: The online media monitor on Climate Change (OMM), Bruggemann and Sadikni (2020))

decrease from January 2020, and settling back to values similar to those before 2018 from April 2020.

These tendencies illustrate that the trend towards deeper environmental concern, associated with growing affluence in the middle class, is not irreversible. Abrupt changes of attention happen, when another issue unexpectedly emerges that is perceived as significant. An example of this would be the attack in 2001 on the Twin-Towers in New York, which immediately lifted the concern about terrorism to top levels. Similarly, in the summer of 2015, the massive influx of refugees into the EU caused a short-term re-orientation of public attention.

7.4   Climate Change Concerns as a Cultural Phenomenon

The concern that human failures (*our "sins"*), would cause adverse climatic conditions is as old as civilization, it seems, see von Storch and Stehr (2000). In premodern times, religious explanations for deficits of precipitation, or for disastrous summers leading to failing harvests were the standard method to make sense of the world, see, e.g., Kershaw (1973). Through nature, God retaliates for the "sins" of humans. This traditional thinking is still used today. For example, some people attributed the flooding of New Orleans to God's judgement over the abortion-clinics in that city. Likewise, The Guardian (2014) reported how some people blamed the 2014-flooding in the UK to the acquiescence to same-sex marriages. In modern times, the same revenge/punishment mechanism is often claimed to be at work, although "God" may be replaced by "Nature".

This idea of retaliation is a Western pattern of thinking, and research on these topics from those in other cultures would be interesting to have. However, given the dominance of post-colonial Western thinking, the Western ideas may also prevail in other parts of the world, even if possibly in a weaker form. In an analysis of coastal flooding in Ghana, such flooding was mostly understood as an "act of God", but without the interpretation of it being sent as a punishment, see Evadzi et al. (2018).

The concept of climate change as a response to human misdoings, is age-old and seems to be an integral part of our culture. Because of this, it can be resurface at any time, with silent public acceptance. A sample of related conversations may therefore sound like this: *"We knew it all along, but it is good that science is now confirming it."*

7.5   Challenges for Obtaining Efficient Interventions

The public, and especially the middle class, is keen on acting against the detrimental scenarios of catastrophic climate change becoming real. While industry, traffic and lifestyles of others are considered the main culprits for the pending disaster, people also want to contribute to the solution by individual action. This wish manifests itself in a large variety of activities, of which many serve other purposes, such as animal health, undisturbed neighbourhoods, air quality, noise disturbances near airports, etcetera. These are often presented as measures to help combat the climate problem, because they could lead to "large" reductions of emissions. However, even though these reductions may appear large when presented in terms of tons of emissions impact, in reality, they are virtually irrelevant on a global scale. This becomes especially clear when measuring the amount of CO_2 emitted on a global basis, namely about 38 *billion* tons (Gigatons = Gt) of CO2 per year. This is the true target for emissions reduction, all of which must come to an end by 2050 in order to meet the goals of the Paris agreement, see IPCC (2014).

An example of these good-sounding but insignificant initiatives was the claim, published in the Danish middle-class journal Politiken (2020), that sorting waste-textiles would contribute (*"help"*) to limit climate change. While this sorting of waste-textiles may make sense for various reasons, there is hardly any measurable effect on climate-relevant emissions. The actions may contribute to a more sustainable economy, but it would not aid in the combat of climate change in any significant way. Not surprisingly, the article only claims that it would "help", and does not quantify it any further.

Obviously, it is difficult for the public to understand the sheer size of the challenge. Most people seem to believe that their actions would matter, hoping that others would follow their good example, which is then assumed to become effective as the sum of all the individual actions. Simple calculations, however, often show that this still does not lead to reductions in the gigaton-range.

The IPCC summarizes the conditions for reaching the Paris goal, of limiting the increase of global mean temperature to 1.5 °C until the end of the century, with stationary conditions[1] afterwards. This goal requires that today's emission of anthropogenic CO_2 of about 38 Gt CO_2/year (*and other greenhouse gases*) is reduced so that the net-emission in 2050 has completely ceased. This has to happen on a planetary scale, everywhere in the world, from all human activities, with subsequent negative emissions in the range of several Gt CO_2/year in the decades to follow.

This simple quantitative assertion is generally not understood by the public, nor by well-meaning, concerned civil society, such as the Fridays for Future movement. They are seriously worried about or even scared of the perspective of future manmade climate "catastrophes". The task is daunting, but instead of asking 'how can this be achieved', populistic requests are aired, to reach these goals of net-zero emissions much earlier, say for Hamburg in 2035. For me, it seems that such groups are not necessarily battling anthropogenic climate change, but use its goals as a vehicle to persuade society to achieve other middle-class goals, in particular to a healthier and supposedly happier life of its members.

The fact that achieving the goal of net-zero emissions requires all societies in the world to adopt it has already been formally accepted by almost all governments of the world. Even so, present efforts do not indicate that we will achieve this goal.[2] This is not really surprising, because the societies and countries of the world face with a variety of challenges, of which climate change is just one. Competition for attention and investment include the previously-mentioned existential worries about food, housing, labour, education and health – commensurate with the fact that many in the world have not yet made it to middle class. The traditional social-democratic issues only lose significance for those who made it into middle class: no poverty, zero hunger, good health and well-being, with a high quality of education, as the United Nations (2015) puts it.

I believe that unorganized citizen activity will not lead to success, not even partial success. We, and the question is of course who "we" are, need to do something else to limit the detrimental climatic effects of ongoing emissions of greenhouse gases into the atmosphere, without neglecting or belittling existing UN development goals for basic well-being and development. For this, we have a tool: the goodwill and intention of the Western middle-class. This tool therefore needs to be focused on the most effective measures, which will likely include other development goals as well.

---

[1] "Stationary conditions" = the temperature varies around this value with relatively small deviations, but there is no systematic in- or decrease.

[2] According to https://climateactiontracker.org/countries/, only two countries are presently underway to meet their Paris obligations: Morocco and Gambia. The EU is classified as "insufficient". [As of 26. August 2020.]

7.6   Focusing the Goodwill of the Western Middle-Class: Apollo Projects

On 12 September 1962, John F Kennedy announced his Apollo project: *"We choose to go to the Moon in this decade ..., not because [it is] easy, but because [it is] hard; because that goal will serve to organize and measure the best of our energies and skills, because that challenge is one that we are willing to accept, one we are unwilling to postpone, and one we intend to win...."*. He suggested to bundle the potential and the will of the United States and its people to do something difficult to achieve. And he added a date: within 10 years. A challenging problem-oriented technological feat, a specific timing and an opportunity for all Americans to be proud of.

Can we think of developing such problem-oriented technologies within a specific time frame, which would allow the middle class take ownership of and be proud in? I would say, 'Yes, we can.' We could suggest that, based on technological expertise, over the next 10 years, Germany could work to develop emission-free ship propulsion; France could do the same with regards to air traffic; and China could work on the electrification of chemical process heat. For further example, Russia could work on the electrification of heating and cooling; and Tanzania could work on providing renewable energy for rural African regions.[3] All of this could be done without compromising the basic development goals of eliminating hunger and poverty, provisioning health and education.

By starting such projects, with the positive attitude of "we can do this" and "we will do it", a constructive combination of the moral inclinations of families, companies and governments for an efficient "stewardship of the natural environment and the climate" may be achieved.

Clearly, even without new middle-class driven and financed Apollo-projects, efforts towards emissions-free technologies are underway in various quarters of science and companies. Governments make big investments into such efforts – but it seems the success is slow. Taking the suggested "Apollo-projects" approach will help bring about both the needed acceleration and scale to the initiatives already on the table to reduce greenhouse gas emissions.

The new Apollo-challenge can be financed by the middle class who eagerly wants to contribute to solving the climate problem, but does not know exactly how to assist or engage. Until now, the middle classes of various countries are spreading goodwill and money for various symbolic acts with no or little gigaton-range effect. The Apollo-challenge targets are visions that can will convince the rest of the world that we are serious. Not by self-acclaimed moral superiority but by economic power, so that everywhere in the world large chunks of emissions of greenhouse gases are phased out – with net-effects in the gigaton-range.

For the sake of clarity, a brief account of the challenge of heating and cooling may be useful. In the EU, the total annual amount of emissions related to heating and cooling is about 1 gigaton of CO_2/year. If sufficient electrical energy is

---

[3] Much better attributions may be possible; this list a mere illustration of what is meant.

available, this process could be transformed to run on electricity without emissions. For this transformation, the energy supply must be safe and reliable. However, there are also practical considerations, such as allowing large housing companies (*such as SAGA in Hamburg*) the ongoing utilization of older and often culturally valuable buildings and locations. Regardless of the opportunities or challenges, for technologies such as these to spread around the world, they need to first and foremost be economically attractive. Only then can the smaller achievements of avoiding several megatons of emissions on a local basis may become an efficient emission reduction in the multi-gigaton range on a global scale.

7.7 Conclusion

In this chapter I have suggested that the goodwill of the middle class in the area climate change is often misguided towards symbolic acts that do not contribute to the real problem of reducing emissions efficiently. Moreover, the attention span of the public might not be long enough that would be needed for a sustained focus on small-scale improvements.

Therefore, I suggest national – or pan-national – projects, for development of technologies that are, first: economically attractive, to be accepted everywhere in the world, and second: effective in making emissions obsolete in sectors which today cause large amounts of emissions, such as traffic, heating and cooling, agriculture and industry. These projects could be financed by tax on the affluent, thereby giving the middle class the feeling that it is taking responsibility and the pride for the great task of making the world a better place.

Another great American declared "*I have a dream*", and surely, the national and pan-national cooperative Apollo-challenges of today are a dream. We need politicians who are able to balance the various interests, cultural frames and short-term economic boundaries. We also need to organize the difficult social and political processes. We need enthusiastic and competent engineers. And, most of all, we need the middle class with its willingness to engage for a common good.

References

Brüggemann, M., & Sadikni, R. (2020). *Online media monitor on climate change (OMM): Analysis of global tweets and online media coverage*. Universität Hamburg. https://icdc.cen.uni-hamburg.de/omm/world.html. Accessed 6 May 2021
Evadzi, P., Scheffran, J., Zorita, E., & Hünicke, B. (2018). Awareness of sea-level response under climate change on the coast of Ghana. *Journal of Coastal Conservation, 22*(1), 183–197.
IPCC. (2014). *Climate change 2014. Synthesis report summary for policymakers*. UN Intergovernmental Panel on Climate Change. https://www.ipcc.ch/site/assets/uploads/2018/02/AR5_SYR_FINAL_SPM.pdf

Kershaw, I. (1973). The great famine and agrarian crisis in England 1315-1322. *Past & Present, 59*, 3–50.

Mandavilli, A. (2020). In N.Y.C.'s Spring Virus Surge, a Frightening Echo of 1918 Flu, *New York Times*, 13 August 2020. https://www.nytimes.com/2020/08/13/health/coronavirus-flu-new-york.html. Accessed 15 Aug 2020.

Neiman, S. (2019). *Learning from the Germans. Confronting race and the memory of Evil.* Farrar Straus & Giroux.

NOS. (2020). *Ruime meerderheid van Nederlanders denkt dat het klimaat verandert*, 17 January 2020. https://nos.nl/artikel/2319094-ruime-meerderheid-van-nederlanders-denkt-dat-het-klimaat-verandert.html

Politiken. (2020). Tøjsortering kan hjælpe klimaet, *Politiken*, 16 August 2020, p. 14.

Radkau, J. (2011). *Die Ära der Ökologie. Eine Weltgeschichte.* CH Beck.

Resch, T., Waibel, M., & Kittel, B. (2020). *Corona, Umwelt, Klima & Nachhaltigkeit*, 3 July 2020. https://viecer.univie.ac.at/corona-blog/corona-blog-beitraege/blog63/. Accessed on 15 Aug 2020.

The Guardian. (2014).*UK storms are divine retribution for gay marriage laws, says UKIP councilor*, 18. January 2014.

United Nations. (2015). *The social development goals.* Obtained from https://sdgs.un.org/goals, as of 20 August 2020.

von Storch, H., & Stehr, N. (2000). Climate change in perspective. Our concerns about global warming have an age-old resonance. *Nature, 405*, 615.

Wahnbaeck, C. (2020). Junge fürchten den Klimawandel mehr als das Virus, *Der Spiegel*, 17.04.2020. https://www.spiegel.de/wirtschaft/leben-mit-corona-umfrage-junge-fuerchten-klimawandel-mehr-als-corona-a-21f6a7f4-8f7e-479f-8c0a-d0c547c3e4ed

Hans von Storch is a German climate scientist and lead author of the 3rd and 5th assessment-report of the IPCC, the UN's climate panel. He is a Professor at the University of Hamburg, and was until 2016 Director of the Institute for Coastal Research at the Helmholtz Helmholtz Zentrum Geesthacht (now Helmholtz Zentrum Hereon, earlier: GKSS Research Center) in Geesthacht, Germany. He is a member of the advisory boards of, among others, the Journal of Climate and editor-in-chief of Oxford University Press Research Encyclopedia Climate Science. He holds a honorary doctorate of the University of Gothenburg, and is a foreign member of the Polish Academy of Sciences, as well as a guest professor at the Ocean University of China. He is a recipient of the order of the Federal Republic of Germany.

Several joined in a critical assessment of the manuscript, thanks to PT, JF, EZ, AWH, RG, AS, HV and RH. The chapter was completed on 1. September 2020; minor clarifications were added in November 2020.

The manufacturer's authorised representative in the EU is Springer
Nature Customer Service Centre GmbH, Europaplatz 3, 69115 Heidelberg,
Germany. If you have any concerns regarding our products, please
contact ProductSafety@springernature.com

Printed and bound by CPI Group (UK) Ltd, Croydon, CR0 4YY

29/04/2026

02099458-0012